MARTIN GILBERT

WINSTON CHURCHILL'S WAR LEADERSHIP

Sir Martin Gilbert is Winston Churchill's official biographer and a leading historian of the modern world. He is the author of seventy-three books, among them *Churchill: A Life*, comprehensive studies of both the First and Second World Wars, and his three-volume work *A History of the Twentieth Century.* He was made an Honorary Fellow of Merton College, Oxford, in 1994, and was knighted in 1995. He lives in London with his wife, Susan, and their two boys.

ALSO BY MARTIN GILBERT

Churchill: A Life

In Search of Churchill: A Historian's Journey

The First World War: A Complete History

The Second World War: A Complete History

A History of the Twentieth Century, Volume I: 1900-1933

A History of the Twentieth Century, Volume II: 1933-1951

A History of the Twentieth Century, Volume III: 1952-1999

Holocaust: The History of the Jews of Europe During the Second World War

The Righteous: The Unsung Heroes of the Holocaust

WINSTON CHURCHILL'S WAR LEADERSHIP

MARTIN GILBERT

VINTAGE BOOKS
A Division of Random House, Inc.
New York

FIRST VINTAGE BOOKS EDITION, APRIL 2004

 Published in the United States by Vintage Books, a division of Random House, Inc., New York. Originally published by Vintage Canada, a division of Random House of Canada Ltd., in 2004.

The Cataloging-in Publication Data is on file at the Library of Congress.

Vintage ISBN: 1-4000-7732-X

www.vintagebooks.com

Printed in the United States of America
10 9 8 7 6 5 4 3 2 1

The problem is not winning the war,
but persuading people to let you win it.

—Winston S. Churchill

WINSTON CHURCHILL'S WAR LEADERSHIP

Introduction

In February 2002 I was asked to speak in the White House about Churchill's war leadership. I was invited into the Oval Office, where I showed the President the bust of Churchill that had recently been presented to him by the British Embassy in Washington, and to which he had given pride of place. As the twenty-first century began, a President of the United States was embarking on two military expeditions, the first against Afghanistan and the second against Iraq—not unlike the British punitive expeditions a century earlier, in which Churchill had taken part.

In the second of those early-twenty-first-century expeditions, the one against Iraq, a British Prime Minister joined the United States with commitment and conviction. The Anglo-American war effort against Iraq involved every aspect of war leadership in a small conflict, even though it will be at least a decade before the real stories of that leadership will begin to emerge through the archives of the conflict: the true nature of the Anglo-American link, the Secret Intelligence dimension, the actual relationship between the leaders and their Ministers and advisers, and the precise pattern of decision-making and execution of orders.

These are important matters for recent history, but

they are minor compared with the leadership aspects of the Second World War. Unlike the Iraqi adversary in 2003, the German enemy sixty years earlier was able to sustain a ferocious aerial bombardment for more than two years, to sustain a devastating submarine offensive for three years, and to fight tenaciously in the field for more than five years. In addition, Germany was able to acquire, after two years of victorious fighting, a remorseless ally: Japan.

War leadership during the Second World War required intensive concentration and decision-making over a lengthy period, filled with dangers and uncertainties on a scale that has not been repeated since then, even in Korea and Vietnam, harsh and prolonged though those conflicts were. In that regard, Churchill's war leadership can have no parallel, unless the world plunges back into a disaster of epic proportions, in which an added dimension could well be the nuclear one.

Leadership against global terrorism requires qualities of a different order, which even now are being formulated and put into practice. In the hope that there may still be some aspects of Churchill's war leadership that can be of service in the present conflict, this book is dedicated to President George W. Bush and Prime Minister Tony Blair.

WHEN WINSTON CHURCHILL BECAME Prime Minister on 10 May 1940, he had been a Member of Parliament for almost forty years. For more than twenty-five of those years he had held high ministerial office, with responsibilities that covered many spheres of national policy and international affairs. Central to the strength of his war leadership was this experience. Churchill could draw upon knowledge acquired in the many fierce political battles and tough international negotiations in which he had been a central and often successful participant. "My knowledge, which has been bought, not taught," was how he expressed it in the House of Commons during a stormy interwar debate on defence.

Churchill's knowledge had often been bought at the price of unpopularity and failure. But, above all, it was the experience of dealing, both as a Cabinet Minister from 1905 and as a member of the Committee of Imperial Defence from 1909, with a wide range of national and world issues, and also of persuading a frequently hostile House of Commons to accept the logic and argument of government policy. That experience served as an essential underpinning—and strengthening—of his leadership in the Second World War. For a decade before the First World War, four Prime Ministers—Campbell-Bannerman, Asquith, Lloyd George and Baldwin—each entrusted Churchill with contentious issues, having a high regard for his negotiating and persuasive skills. The experience he gained was considerable. In 1911 he had been a pioneer of industrial conciliation and arbitration at a time of intense labour unrest. In 1913 he had led the search for an amelioration of Anglo-German naval rivalry. In 1914 his duties as First Lord of the Admiralty (the post he was to hold again on the outbreak of war in 1939) included both the air defence of London and the protection of the Royal Navy and merchant shipping from German naval attack. In 1917 he was put in charge of munitions production in Britain at a time of the greatest need and strain. In 1919 he devised, as a matter of urgency, a system of demobilization that calmed the severe tensions of a disaffected soldiery. In the early 1920s he had been at the centre of resolving the demands of Irish Catholics for Home Rule and of the first—and effectively the last—border delineation dispute between Southern Ireland and Ulster. At the same time, he had undertaken the complicated task of carrying out Britain's promise to the Jews of a National Home in Palestine after the First World War.

This experience of dealing at the centre with Britain's major national needs, during more than three decades, gave Churchill a precious boon from the first days of his premiership. It also provided him with many specific pointers to war direction. A quarter of a century before he became Prime Minister, he had seen the perils that accompanied the evolution of war policy when there was no central direction. He had been a member of the War Council in 1914, when the Prime Minister, Asquith, had been unable to exercise effective control over the two Service departments—the army and the navy. To redress this problem, on becoming Prime Minister in May 1940, Churchill created the post, hitherto unknown in Britain, of Minister of Defence. Although the new Ministry had no departmental structure as such, it did have a secretariat, headed by General Hastings Ismay, who served, with his small staff, as a direct conduit between the Prime Minister and the Chiefs of Staff—the respective heads of the army, navy and air force. This structure enabled Churchill to put forward his suggestions directly, and with the utmost directness, to those who would have to accept or reject, modify and implement them.

The organization of his wartime premiership was a central feature of Churchill's war leadership. That organization took several months to perfect, but from his first days as Prime Minister and Minister of Defence he worked to establish it, and to create in the immediate ambit of 10 Downing Street an organization that would give the nation strong and effective leadership. At its core was the close relationship between Churchill and the three Chiefs of Staff. Their frequent meetings, often daily, enabled him to discuss with them the many crises of the war, to tackle the many emergencies, and to decide on an acceptable common strategy. Working under the Chiefs of Staff, and in close association with Churchill through the Ministry of Defence, were two other essential instruments of military planning: the Joint Planning Staff (known as the "Joint Planners") and the Joint Intelligence Committee.

Other essential elements of the organizational side of Churchill's war leadership evolved as the need arose, among them the Production Council, the Import Executive, the Tank Parliament, the Combined Raw Materials Board (an Anglo-America venture), the Anglo-American Shipping Adjustment Board, and the Battle of the Atlantic Committee of the War Cabinet. And always to hand was the apparatus of Intelligence gathering, assessment and distribution, controlled by the Secret Intelligence Services headed by Colonel (later General) Stewart Menzies, with whom Churchill was in daily communication. In his Minutes to Menzies, Churchill made whatever comments he felt were needed on the nature, implications and circulation of Intelligence material.

This organizational structure gave Churchill a method of war leadership whereby the highest possible accumulation of professional knowledge was at his disposal. He was not a dictatorial leader, although he could be emphatic in his requests and suggestions. If the Chiefs of Staff opposed any initiative he proposed, it was abandoned. He had no power to overrule their collective will. But on most occasions there was no such stark dichotomy. He and they were searching for the same outcome—the means, first, to avert defeat; then to contain and, finally, to defeat Germany—and in this search they were in frequent agreement.

One of the members of Churchill's Private Office, John Peck, later recalled: "I have the clearest possible recollection of General Ismay talking to me about a meeting of the Chiefs of Staff Committee at which they got completely stuck and admitted that they just did not know what was the right course to pursue; so on a purely military matter, they had come to Churchill, civilian, for his advice. He introduced some further facts into the equation that had escaped their notice and the solution became obvious."

A crucial aspect of Churchill's war leadership was his private secretariat, the Private Office at 10 Downing Street. Members of his Private Office accompanied him wherever he went, whether in Britain or overseas, and were available to help smooth his path during every working hour, often until late into the night. At its centre were his Private Secretaries: civil servants, mostly in their thirties, who remained at his side on a rota system throughout the week and the weekend. They were privy to his innermost thoughts (although not, ironically, to the decrypted Enigma messages on which so many of those thoughts hinged). They knew how to interpret his briefest of instructions, some of which were scarcely more than a grunt or a nod of the head. They knew how to find documents and to circulate them. They kept his desk diary with its myriad appointments. They also ensured that whatever the Prime Minister needed—a document to study, a file to scrutinize, a colleague to question, a journey to be organized, a foreign dignitary to be received—all was ready at the right time and in the right place. Given the scale of Churchill's travel in Britain and overseas, and his notorious unpunctuality and indecision in little things, this streamlined operation was impressive. In a private letter to General Sir Bernard Montgomery, Clementine Churchill referred to her husband's "chronic unpunctuality" and "habit of changing his mind (in little things) every minute!" For example, his Private Secretariat was caused endless vexation as to whether he would receive some important visitor at 10 Downing Street, at No. 10 Annexe a hundred yards away, or in the Prime Minister's room in the House of Commons.

Churchill could also show uncertainty regarding the large decisions, rehearsing them in his mind and hesitating for long periods before settling on a course of action. One such instance was the difficult decision, which he supported, to send British troops to Greece to take part in the defence of that country against a possible German attack, thus weakening the British forces that were then defending Egypt. In the end, he asked for every member of his War Cabinet to vote on this matter. The unanimous vote was in favour of showing Greece that she was not to be abandoned by her ally, despite the hopelessness of the situation, given German military superiority.

The names of most of the members of Churchill's

Private Office are little known to history. Only one, John Colville—who started as the Junior Private Secretary in 1940—subsequently made his mark, one of great importance to history, because he kept a detailed diary (quite against the rules) of those days when he was on duty. Neither the first Principal Private Secretary, Eric Seal, nor Seal's successor John Martin, nor the other members of the Private Office—John Peck, Christopher Dodds and Leslie Rowan—kept anything more than a few jottings and private letters. The whole team constituted, collectively, the support system on which Churchill depended and from whom he obtained first-class service, ensuring the smooth running of the prime ministerial enterprise at its centre. The members of his Private Office sustained him without publicity or fanfare, but with a professionalism and a devotion that helped to make his leadership both smooth and effective.

One integral part of the Private Office were the secretary-typists—a lynchpin of the whole vast operation. At their apex was a woman whose photograph at Churchill's side almost never appeared in the press. Her name was Kathleen Hill. She had been his residential secretary since 1936. Once, at the end of the war, when a newspaper published a photograph of Churchill which included her walking next to him, she was described in the caption as "an unknown woman." Her contribution to Churchill's war leadership was silent, unnoticed and essential.

The method used by Churchill and Mrs. Hill, and by his two other principal typists, Elizabeth Layton and Marian Holmes, was simple and effective. They would sit "still as a mouse" (in Mrs. Hill's words) wherever Churchill was, whether in Downing Street, at his country retreat at Chequers, travelling by car, on trains, on board ship, even on planes, with a notepad at the ready or with a silent typewriter (specially designed by Remington), paper in place, to take down whatever he might say whenever he might say it. He might be reading a newspaper and be prompted by something he read to dictate a Minute to a Cabinet Minister. He might be reading a clutch of diplomatic telegrams from ambassadors overseas, or top-secret signals from commanders-in-chief on land, sea or air, and have a thought, a point of criticism, a note of praise, a request for information, or a suggestion for action. As he began to speak, often in a difficult mumble, the typist on duty would immediately take down his words and transcribe them. So good was this trio of Mrs. Hill, Miss Layton and Miss Holmes that, after one or another of them had taken down his words on the silent typewriter as he spoke them, all that remained was to hand him the sheet of paper for his signature. They were masters of their craft. A fourth member of this team was Churchill's shorthand writer Patrick Kinna. It was he who had been present when Churchill, walking naked in his bedroom at the White House after a bath, giving dictation, was interrupted by President Roosevelt, who entered the room. Churchill, "never being lost for words," as Kinna recalled, said, "You see, Mr. President, I have nothing to conceal from you."

There can hardly have been a single day of the war when Churchill did not dictate to one or other of his devoted secretarial staff. At the outset of his premiership, he decided that every instruction, suggestion, proposal or criticism emanating from him—and all the answers he received—should be in writing. He remembered too many occasions during the First World War when a policy agreed upon at one meeting was challenged at the next but there was no written record to show what the first decision had been or what arguments had been put forward and by whom, either for it or against. He was determined that no such muddles and uncertainties would exist under his war leadership. "Let it be clearly understood," he minuted on 19 July 1940, to General Ismay, as well as to the Cabinet Secretary, Sir Edward Bridges, and the Chief of the Imperial Staff, Field Marshal Sir John Dill, "that all directions emanating from me are made in writing, or should be immediately afterwards confirmed in writing, and that I do not accept any responsibility for matters relating to national defence, on which I am alleged to have given directions, unless they are given in writing." This Minute was shown to all members of Churchill's Private Office and implemented.

In March 1918, during the First World War crisis when German forces drove back the Anglo-French defenders and confusion and doubt reigned among the British war leadership, Churchill wrote to the Prime Minister, Lloyd George: "Ponder—and then act" (Churchill underlined the word *act*). The equivalent instruction in the Second World War, often given a dozen times or more each day, was "Action This Day." It would accompany a written Minute—the basic method of communication between the Prime Minister and those he needed to consult—sent from Churchill to Ismay for the Chiefs of Staff or direct from Churchill to the Cabinet Minister responsible. For urgent Minutes, Churchill's Private Office stuck on a brightly coloured label with "Action This Day" printed on it. The combination of intense thought and consultation, followed by a clear instruction for action, enabled the war machinery to advance. Every time Churchill minuted his thoughts, concerns and instructions, that machinery moved one step forward.

The Private Office devised a system whereby Churchill could have everything he needed at his fingertips. That system revolved around the Prime Minister's traditional locked boxes that went with him—or were brought to him by messenger—wherever he might be: at 10 Downing Street; at Chequers; at his most frequented base, the above-ground secret wartime "Number Ten Annexe" (one floor above the underground Cabinet War Rooms); in the Cabinet War Rooms themselves whenever they were used during an air raid; and during travels throughout Britain and overseas. Churchill devised the arrangement of the boxes himself, a system, John Peck commented, "peculiarly Winston's own, and it was in a sense the nerve centre of his war effort." Inside the box, the first set of folders was marked "Top of the Box" and contained those items, covering every aspect of the war effort, considered by the Private Office to be particularly urgent. The next set of folders was labelled "Foreign Office Telegrams": Churchill liked to follow closely what the ambassadors were sending and what they were being sent. Then came "Service Telegrams," the exchanges between the three Service Ministers and the principal commanders in the field. Next were "Periodical Returns." As Peck explained: "He was keenly interested in the development of new equipment. He was also much concerned about the necessity for speed and punctuality in delivery despite bombing, breakdown and other causes of delay." These Periodical Returns included monthly, weekly and even—where Churchill considered them necessary—daily reports on production, technical developments, manpower, training, tank and aircraft strengths, and much else. They enabled Churchill to make sure, as Peck expressed it, "that there were no disasters due to lack of zeal or direction in the back rooms."

Also in the daily budget of locked boxes—in addition to the buff-coloured boxes containing Secret Intelligence material and material from the Joint Intelligence Committee, to which Churchill alone had the key—were files on parliamentary questions that Churchill had to answer, letters for signature, a folder marked "To See" with items that his Private Office thought he would be interested in, a special file from General Ismay with reports from the Chiefs of Staff, and a folder of documents that Churchill himself had marked "R Week-end": things he wanted to be returned to him at the weekend when he would have more time to study them.

Churchill worked through his boxes every morning, before he got out of bed; every evening, often until late into the night if the material in the boxes made such working necessary; and throughout the weekends—generating a stream of Minutes of his own, seeking information. Often he would mark on a document the instruction "Ismay to explain" or "Prof Lindemann to advise" on some statistic; or, on one occasion at least, the single word "elucidate."

The pressure of work on any British Prime Minister, let alone a wartime Prime Minister, is formidable. (I once spent an evening watching John Major working his way through his boxes in the flat at Downing Street. As soon as he had finished going through one box, with all its challenges and burdens, another was brought up to him, and so on, from early evening until midnight.) While Churchill's daily life had to centre upon the demands of the war, he was also conscious of the need to lead as normal and as sustaining a life as possible. One rule he insisted upon from the outset of his premiership: when he had gone to bed at night he was not to be woken up by any news, however bad, except the invasion of Britain.

His pattern of daily life was as fixed as the circumstances of war allowed. Each morning he stayed in bed as long as possible, working and dictating from a wooden tray that had been specially designed to hold his books and papers. He got up only when he was needed at a meeting—usually the Chiefs of Staff in mid-morning or the War Cabinet at noon. He saw no point in rising if there was no need to do so. His Private Office and his typists were used to him working in bed and adjusted their activities accordingly: there was certainly no falling off of effort and productivity. Each afternoon, usually at about five o'clock, he would return to bed, burrow inside the sheets, and have an hour or so of deep sleep before he got up and embarked on his work again, refreshed. By this means he effectively created for himself a two-day working day.

Each night before going to bed, or each morning before getting up, he would read all the main newspapers—nine or ten in all—absorbing the way the public were being informed about the war, studying the editorials, and looking through news items that alerted him to myriad aspects of the daily life of the nation. Did a reduction in the food ration seem to be creating public hostility? A brief request from Churchill to Professor Lindemann, head of the Downing Street Statistical Branch—a branch of Churchill's inner war-policy grouping containing eight university statisticians—would ascertain the facts of the situation (the ration itself, the reserves of whatever food or other rationed item it was, the supply and import situation). Then Churchill would dictate a Minute to the Minister of Food or some other Ministers concerned, asking for more facts and suggesting an amelioration. Much of the thrust of Churchill's reading of the newspapers was to reduce hardships and grievances among the public, especially factory workers, servicemen and -women, and their families. Two examples: Reading of a prison sentence imposed on a woman who had compared him to Hitler, Churchill insisted on the sentence being reduced. He did likewise when he read of a group of firemen who had been on duty during a night of severe bombing, and been heavily fined for "looting" some bottles of wine and spirits from a bombed-out pub.

Churchill's leadership and his moods were closely interwoven. He was not enamoured of harsh words and conflict. On one occasion he told a visitor: "Anger is a waste of energy. Steam, which is used to blow off a safety valve, would be better used to drive an engine." But the strains of leadership were enormous, and he often turned to anger and petulance. His wife, Clementine, saw this tension in the dire summer of 1940 and was fearless in her criticism; she felt she alone could raise the issue, knowing that her husband had the strength of character to accept blame and to act upon it. On one occasion that summer she warned him that "a devoted friend" in his inner circle had reported to her a decline in his character. After setting out some of the details of what she had heard, including his being "so contemptuous" at conferences "that presently no ideas, good or bad, will be forthcoming," she added: "My darling Winston—I must confess that I have noticed a deterioration in your manner; & you are not so kind as you used to be. It is for you to give the Orders, & if they are bungled . . . you can sack anyone & everyone. Therefore with this terrific power you must combine urbanity, kindness & if possible Olympic calm."

Recalling how she was accustomed to hearing praise from all those who had worked with him, Clementine Churchill told her husband that those to whom she had spoken about his new-found irritability had commented: "No doubt it's the strain." There was truth in that. "You must indeed have had a terrible time during the last fortnight," the British Ambassador in Madrid, Sir Samuel Hoare—a former Conservative Cabinet colleague—wrote to him a week later. The slow pace of vital United States supplies, the imminent collapse of France, and the prospect of a German invasion of Britain were all heavy burdens on Churchill at that time.

Churchill did heed his wife's admonition, although future setbacks and burdens saw that irascibility return: many wartime diarists give evidence of that. They also reveal his ability, even in difficult times, to assert his charm, his forbearance and his generosity of spirit. General Sir Alan Brooke, who was to record in his diary many moments when Churchill was angry and cantankerous, also saw the thoughtful, calm, courageous side of his character. "Just by ourselves at the end of a long day's work and rather trying," Brooke noted on 23 July 1940. "But he was very nice and I got a good insight into the way his brain is working. He is most interesting to listen to and full of marvellous courage considering the burden his is bearing." The American Ambassador in Britain, Gilbert Winant, later recalled Churchill's mood immediately after Pearl Harbor, when the two men had been together at Chequers and Churchill feared that the United States would focus all its efforts on the war in the Pacific, and leave Britain to fight in Europe alone: "He knew at that moment that his country might be 'hanging on one turn of pitch and toss.' Nevertheless he turned to me with the charm of manner that I saw in difficult moments, and said, 'We're late, you know. You get washed and we will go in to lunch together.'"

Churchill's typists were also to find that, however bad his moods could be in dire moments of the war, he always had words of comfort for them and a ready smile—his "beatific grim," as Marian Holmes called it. "Don't mind me," he would say after an outburst, "it's not you—it's the war." On one occasion, in November 1944, finding Marian Holmes and her colleague Elizabeth Layton working in the Hawtrey Room at Chequers without a fire, he commented, "Oh, you poor things. You must light a fire and get your coats. It's just as well I came in"—and he proceeded to light the fire himself, piling it high with logs.

"There is no defeat in his heart": with these words the Australian Prime Minister Robert Menzies summed up in his diary a central feature—if not the dominant and crucial feature—of Churchill's leadership. Defeatism, fear, uncertainty, and the attractions of a negotiated or a compromise peace all bedeviled the first six months of the war, and even later months as the recurring crises of the war looked grim for Britain. Even when he could see no way forward, however, Churchill combatted all defeatist tendencies with total determination. When one of his closest friends, "Bendor," Duke of Westminster, told a group of friends that the war was part of a Jewish and Masonic plot to destroy Christian civilization, Churchill warned in a private letter marked "secret and personal": "I am sure that pursuit of this line would lead you into measureless odium and vexation. When a country is fighting a war of this kind, very hard experiences lie before those who preach defeatism and set themselves against the will of the nation."

One fear Churchill had in the summer of 1940 was that the public would find evidence that the government was planning for the possibility of defeat. He was determined to give a lead in eliminating any evidence to that effect. Plans had been put forward by the Foreign Office for the evacuation of the Royal Family and the government (including Churchill) to "some part of the Overseas Empire, where the war would continue to be waged." As soon as this suggestion reached Churchill, he wrote to one of his trusted advisers: "I believe we shall make them rue the day they tried to invade our island. No such discussion can be permitted." On the following day Churchill was asked if he would authorize sending the paintings in the National Gallery from London to Canada. His answer was succinct: "No, bury them in caves and cellars. None must go. We are going to beat them."

Nineteen days after Churchill became Prime Minister, as British troops were falling back towards Dunkirk, the Italian government indicated its willingness to mediate between Britain and Germany, with a view to some form of negotiated peace. Churchill was certain that the only terms Britain could acquire from a triumphant Germany would be those of subordination and servitude. At the least, Germany had intimated that it must be allowed to retain its conquests in the east: Prague and Warsaw were both under German rule. At that very moment, British troops were fighting in France to try to prevent a German victory there, and British airmen were combatting the German air force above French soil. Churchill could not conceive of negotiations doing anything except seal the fate of France, and undermine the British resolve to fight on once France had surrendered. Yet, at four in the afternoon of May 29, in a meeting held in Churchill's room in the House of Commons, the British Foreign Secretary, Lord Halifax, told the War Cabinet: "We must not ignore the fact that we might get better terms before France went out of the war and our aircraft factories were bombed, than we might get in three months time."

Churchill, in the strongest assertion of his war leadership yet seen, or required, opposed this line of reasoning. The notes of the War Cabinet recorded his response: "It was impossible to imagine that Herr Hitler would be so foolish as to let us continue our rearmament. In effect, his terms would put us completely at his mercy. We should get no worse terms if we went on fighting, even if we were beaten, than were open to us now. If, however, we continued the war and Germany attacked us, no doubt we should suffer some damage, but they also would suffer severe losses. Their oil supplies might be reduced. A time might come when we felt that we had to put an end to the struggle, but the terms would not then be more mortal than those offered to us now." Both Halifax and Neville Chamberlain—whom Churchill had brought into his War Cabinet—saw some merit in saying (as Chamberlain expressed it) "that, while we would fight to the end to preserve our independence, we were ready to consider decent terms if such were offered to us."

Churchill believed that this willingness to consider "decent terms" was a misreading of the public mood, but he could not know for certain, and he had no veto on any majority decision that might be made against him. At this point in the discussion, however, he had to ask for a break in the War Cabinet meeting—which had already lasted for two hours—to meet, for the first time since he had formed his Government, the twenty-five members of his administration who were not in the inner circle: the Junior Ministers and those Cabinet Ministers who were not in the War Cabinet. That meeting, fixed for six o'clock, had been set up several days earlier. No sooner had these Ministers come into his room in the House of Commons—the War Cabinet having left—than Churchill told them that although Hitler would probably "take Paris and offer terms," as might the Italians too, he, Churchill, had no doubt whatever "that we must decline anything like this and fight on."

To Churchill's surprise, as he spoke the words "fight on," there was a sudden outpouring of support from the twenty-five Ministers assembled there, in the very room where the discussion about a negotiated peace had just taken place. Churchill was overwhelmed by their spontaneous determination for continuing the fight. It gave him the added strength he needed half an hour later, at the reconvened War Cabinet meeting. Referring to the extraordinary enthusiasm he had witnessed for continuing the fight, Churchill went on to win the argument for continuing to resist the Nazi onslaught, telling the War Cabinet, "He did not remember having ever before heard a gathering of persons occupying high places in political life express themselves so emphatically."

One of the Ministers present at the six o'clock meeting, Hugh Dalton—who had just been appointed Minister of Economic Warfare—recorded in his diary the words Churchill used in the moments leading up to the sudden demonstration of support for continuing the war. "I am convinced," Churchill told them, "that every man of you would rise up and tear me down from my place if I were for one moment to contemplate parley or surrender. If this long island story of ours is to end at last, let it end only when each one of us lies choking in his own blood upon the ground." Then followed the demonstration of support. Dalton noted in his diary: "Not much more was said. "No one expressed even the faintest flicker of dissent."

Thus Churchill learned that his determination not to surrender reflected a wider mood. He was certain it would be supported by the nation at large, and he immediately wrote one of the strongest official notes of his war premiership, addressed to all Cabinet Ministers and senior civil servants. Marked "Strictly confidential," it was a supreme example of his war leadership, putting to those at the apex of power his implacable opposition to defeatism. "In these dark days," the note read, "the Prime Minister would be grateful if all his colleagues in the Government, as well as high officials, would maintain a high morale in their circles; not minimizing the gravity of events, but showing confidence in our ability and inflexible resolve to continue the war till we have broken the will of the enemy to bring all Europe under his domination. No tolerance should be given to the idea that France will make a separate peace; but whatever may happen on the Continent, we cannot doubt our duty and we shall certainly use all our power to defend the Island, the Empire and our Cause."

The battle against defeatism was not over. On the last day of May, Churchill was shown a seven-page note by the Australian High Commissioner in London, Stanley Bruce, favouring an international conference "to formulate a peace settlement." Churchill struck out this paragraph, writing in the margin a single word: "No." Against another point made by Bruce, that "the further shedding of blood and the continuance of needless suffering is unnecessary" and that the belligerents should "cease the struggle," Churchill wrote the word "Rot." Where Bruce concluded that negotiations were possible, Churchill commented, "The end is rotten."

Churchill tried to prevent any suggestion of defeatism, wherever it emerged. In the summer of 1940 the Admiralty devised a scheme—of which I, aged three and a half, was a part—to evacuate British children to Canada and the United States. Churchill opposed this plan. It only went ahead because the meeting at which it was put before the War Cabinet was interrupted by news of the Franco-German armistice, before any formal decision about the evacuees was reached. "A large movement of this kind," Churchill told the War Cabinet during the discussion, "encourages a defeatist spirit, which was contrary to the true facts of the position and should be sternly discouraged." The Minister concerned went ahead, regardless.

At that same War Cabinet meeting, convened at a time when rumours of an imminent invasion were gaining momentum, the Cabinet invited Churchill to issue a circular to the heads of all government departments, instructing them to take drastic steps to put a stop to defeatist talk. The War Cabinet had just been told by the Intelligence Services, based partly on intercepted private correspondence, that the publication of the most recent deaths from a German air raid—eleven civilians killed and more than a hundred injured in the Newcastle area—might "have a demoralizing effect in the country." To combat this mood, the War Cabinet agreed that Churchill himself should draft and sign a message to be sent to more than three thousand people: to all Members of Parliament, Peers, Lord Lieutenants of the counties of the United Kingdom, Lord Mayors and Privy Councillors—the very centre of British governance. The message, which was printed over a facsimile of Churchill's signature, began: "On what may be the eve of an attempted invasion or battle for our native land, the Prime Minister desires to impress upon all persons holding responsible positions in the Government, in the fighting services or in the civil departments, their duty to maintain a spirit of alert and confident energy."

After setting out his confidence that a German invasion could be repulsed, Churchill continued: "The Prime Minister expects all His Majesty's Servants in high places to set an example of steadiness and resolution. They should check and rebuke expressions of loose and ill-digested opinion in their circles, or by their subordinates. They should not hesitate to report, or if necessary remove, any officers or officials who are found to be consciously exercising a disturbing or depressing influence, and whose talk is calculated alarm and despondency. Thus alone will they be worthy of the fighting men, who in the air, on the sea, and on land have already met the enemy without any sense of being outmatched in martial qualities."

In what was arguably the "finest hour" of Churchill's leadership, he had successfully challenged defeatist talk. Churchill understood that the British people were determined, despite the mounting dangers, to fight on. He commented on one occasion, with regard to the British character and its soundness in adversity: "The British people are like the sea. You can put the bucket in anywhere, and pull it up, and always find it salt." In a speech in the House of Commons on 21 November 1940, bluntly describing the difficulties that lay ahead—"the darker side of our dangers and burdens"—Churchill commented: "I know that it is in adversity that British qualities shine the brightest, and it is under these extraordinary tests that the character of our slowly wrought institutions reveals its latent, invisible strength." In a comment to one of his Private Office about Ernest Bevin, a senior Labour Party figure in his coalition and, as Minister of Labour, the man responsible for the vast wartime workforce, Churchill described him as "a good old thing with the right stuff in him and no defeatist tendencies." It was Churchill's own opposition to all forms of defeatism that marked out the first six months of his war premiership and established the nature and pattern of his war leadership.

Churchill had found the will and the strength to challenge defeatism. All his life he had been an opponent of supine surrender. But there were times, especially when there was news of heavy loss of life at sea or in the air, or in the German bombardment of British cities, when Churchill could be cast down and depressed, albeit briefly. In a speech in the House of Commons shortly before he became Prime Minister, he described these spells as "the brown hours, when baffling news comes, and disappointing news." Yet even when the news was bleak, Churchill found the means to combat depression. In those very "brown hours," he told the Commons on 8 May 1940—when the battle in Norway was going so badly for Britain, provoking a political crisis with Churchill at its centre—"I always turn for refreshment to the reports of the German wireless. I love to read the lies they tell of all the British ships they have sunk so many times over, and to survey the fools' paradise in which they find it necessary to keep their deluded serfs and robots." This attitude was Churchill's nature. It was also what he recognized as an essential feature of successful war leadership: avoiding depression and despair.

During the many periods that still lay ahead, of setbacks on the battlefield or of the relentless German submarine sinkings of British merchant ships in the Atlantic, Churchill's "brown hours" were many. The sinking of the British warships *Prince of Wales* and *Repulse* off Malaya three days after Pearl Harbor was one such time. The fall of Singapore in February 1942 was another. But Churchill never allowed such moments to dominate him or to affect him adversely beyond the moment. After the fall of Singapore, which he admitted to the House of Commons cast "the shadow of a heavy and far-reaching military defeat," he went on to tell the parliamentarians: "Here is the moment to display that calm and poise, combined with grim determination, which not so very long ago brought us out of the very jaws of death"—the Dunkirk evacuation. "Here," Churchill added, "is another occasion to show—as so often in our long story—that we can meet reverses with dignity and with renewed accessions of strength."

As parliamentary criticism of his leadership grew after the fall of Singapore, Churchill confided another of his fears to Roosevelt: "I do not like these days of personal stress and I have found it difficult to keep my eye on the ball." He could not reveal in Parliament the facts as he knew them: that the Commander-in-Chief Far East's report on the fall of Singapore told of "the lack of real fighting spirit" among the troops not only in Malaya but also in Burma, where a Japanese attack was expected at any moment. This information had to remain secret from all but the most inner circle, and it had to be kept from the House of Commons, even though it was both an explanation and a "defence" of what had happened. In the course of the war, Parliament had to take many things on trust; some information was conveyed to it in specially convened Secret Sessions, where Churchill spoke with great frankness, but where the usual parliamentary record was not made public. As Churchill told Roosevelt: "Democracy has to prove that it can provide a granite foundation for war against tyranny."

When, not long after the start of the Japanese war, one of Churchill's staff brought him some particularly grim news, Churchill commented: "We must just KBO." The initials stood for "Keep Buggering On." At other moments of bad news he would burst into a popular music hall song of the First World War, "Keep right on to the end of the road." He even sang this song to Stalin at a time when his Soviet ally suddenly began to accuse him of not really wanting to see the defeat of Hitler. That song, a member of the British delegation explained to a startled generalissimo, "is Britain's secret weapon."

A war leader is only as strong as the information reaching him, and his ability to use that information. A determining factor in Churchill's war leadership was his use of top-secret Intelligence. Some was provided by agents in the field, some by aerial reconnaissance. Information of crucial importance was also gleaned from careful clandestine reading of telegrams sent to and from neutral embassies in London, and from Signals Intelligence of the most secret sort. Several times each day Churchill and his Chiefs of Staff received what Churchill called his "golden eggs"—the intercepted top-secret German radio communications, including many from Hitler himself, transmitted through the Enigma machine. These messages were decrypted at Bletchley Park, northwest of London, by a staff that was to exceed five thousand before the end of the war.

These "golden eggs"—laid, Churchill once remarked, "by the geese who never cackled," the staff at Bletchley—gave Churchill and those in the inner circle an insight, unique in the history of modern warfare, into the strategic thinking and tactical intentions of the enemy. Beyond the staff at Bletchley, the number of people privy to the Enigma decrypts was strictly limited: in September 1940 only thirty-one people within the governing instrument in London were aware of their existence or able to take them into account in policy making. When Churchill learned of a dozen others in receipt of this information, he cut most of them out, minuting to the head of the Secret Intelligence Services: "The wild scattering of secret information must be curbed." Beyond the small group in London—who included King George VI—the others who knew of this most secret source were the land, sea and air commanders-in-chief, to whom the relevant aspects were transmitted, and the Special Liaison Unit officers at the commander-in-chiefs' headquarters, who decoded them.

During the Cold War decades that followed the Second World War, none of the participants in these Enigma-based decisions were able to refer to them in their memoirs, a ban that also applied to Churchill. Secrecy had to be maintained, as the Enigma machine continued to be used by several post-war governments. As a result, both at the time and even as late as the beginning of the twenty-first century, many major British wartime decisions have been seen as absurd, unintelligible, or as the result of Churchill's personal interference. For Churchill, his War Cabinet and the Chiefs of Staff, the Enigma revelations played a crucial role in the process of deciding how to respond and where to strike. Along with its innumerable tactical and strategic benefits, Enigma also revealed some of the innermost decision-making processes of the enemy.

The search for, and achievement of, national unity was another vital aspect of Churchill's war leadership. From the outset of his premiership, Churchill determined to set aside the hostilities and animosities of the pre-war years. For almost a decade he had been the most outspoken critic of the government of the day, castigating it in Parliament, in public and in print for its neglect of national defence. The country had been as divided as its politicians, and vitriol had been the order of the day. From the first days of Churchill's war government, however, those who had been his severest critics, and whom he had most severely criticized, became, at his request, colleagues charged with averting defeat and preserving the realm. A few hours before he became Prime Minister, his son, Randolph, asked whether he would achieve the highest place—arguably his father's ambition for more than thirty years. Churchill replied, "Nothing matters now except beating the enemy."

When he formed his government on 10 May 1940, Churchill was confronted by near outrage among some of his closest friends and allies for giving high positions to former adversaries, including those who had kept him out of office and had belittled his policies on the eve of war. Churchill was emphatic in his reply. "As for me," he wrote to one pre-war adversary who had apologized for his role in trying to remove Churchill from Parliament, "the past is dead." Two days before he became Prime Minister, during the debate in the House of Commons when Chamberlain's leadership and Churchill's conduct of the Norwegian Campaign were both under attack, Churchill appealed to his fellow parliamentarians in these words: "I say, let pre-war feuds die; let personal quarrels be forgotten, and let us keep our hatreds for the common enemy. Let Party interests be ignored, let all our energies be harnessed, let the whole ability and forces of the nation be hurled into the struggle, and let the strong horses be pulling on the collar."

Three months later, as Prime Minister, he was to reiterate this theme with even greater force. After describing the recriminations between France and Britain on the eve of the fall of France as well as the neglect by the pre-war British government to provide an adequate army for fighting on the continent, he told the House of Commons:

> I am not reciting these facts for the purpose of recrimination. That, I judge, to be utterly futile and even harmful. We cannot afford it. I recite them in order to explain why it was that we did not have, as we could have had, between twelve and fourteen British divisions fighting in the line in this great battle instead of only three. Now I put all this aside. I put it on the shelf, from which the

> historians, if they have time, will select their documents and tell their stories. We have to think of the future and not of the past. This also applies in a small way to our own affairs at home. There are too many who would hold an inquest in the House of Commons on the conduct of the Governments—and of Parliaments, for they are in it too—during the years which led up to this catastrophe. They seek to indict those who were responsible for the guidance of our affairs. This also would be a foolish and pernicious process. There are too many in it. Let each man search his conscience and search his speeches. I frequently search mine.

Churchill continued: "Of this I am quite sure, that if we open a quarrel between the past and the present, we shall find that we have lost the future."

Churchill rejected the demand that those who had been at the centre of the pre-war appeasement policy not be rewarded for their pre-war stance. He told the House of Commons: "Every Minister who tries each day to do his duty shall be respected, and their subordinates must know that their chiefs are not threatened men, men who are here today and gone tomorrow, but that their directions must be punctually and faithfully obeyed. Without this concentrated power we cannot face what lies before us."

One of Churchill's ministerial appointments—Captain David Margesson as Chief Whip—was particularly criticized by those who wanted to see the pre-war

"Men of Munich" excluded from government. Margesson had been both Stanley Baldwin's and Neville Chamberlain's Chief Whip, active in helping to keep Churchill out of office and in dragooning the serried ranks of Conservative Members of Parliament to vote against many of his proposals on national defence, including his advocacy of a Ministry of Supply to enable industry to prepare for the eventuality of war. To a Conservative anti-appeasement Member of Parliament who had voiced his opposition to the retention of Margesson, Churchill wrote: "It has been my deliberate policy to try to rally all the forces for the life and death struggle in which we are plunged, and to let bygones be bygones. I am quite sure that Margesson will treat me with the loyalty that he has given to my predecessors." He added: "The fault alleged against him which tells the most is that he has done his duty only too well. I do not think that there is anyone who could advise me better about all those elements in the Tory Party who were so hostile to us in recent years. I have to think of unity, and I need all the strength I can get." As to the Chief Whip's qualities, Churchill wrote, "I have long had a very high opinion of Margesson's administrative and executive abilities." Not long after writing this letter, Churchill appointed Margesson to be Secretary of State for War.

———

At the centre of Churchill's mental energies as war leader was his belief in himself—in his abilities and in his destiny. While at school, he had gathered a group of boys around him and explained his confidence that one day, far in the future, when London was under attack from an invader, he would be in command of the capital's defences. As a young soldier he thought that destiny had somehow marked him out, and he expressed that belief on several occasions in letters to his mother. In 1897, on his way to his first action on the northwest frontier of India, he wrote to her: "I have faith in my star—that I am intended to do something in this world." In 1900, when he was only twenty-six years old but already a participant in three wars and the author of five books, Captain Percy Scott, a naval gunnery expert whom he had met in the Boer War, predicted a remarkable future for him. "I feel certain," wrote Scott, "that I shall some day shake hands with you as Prime Minister of England; you possess the two necessary qualifications, genius and plod. Combined, I believe nothing can keep them back." To Violet Asquith, who had spoken cynically about men in general, Churchill remarked a few years later: "All men are worms, but I do believe that I am a glow worm."

During the first six months of 1916, when Churchill was serving as a battalion commander on the Western Front, a German shell had nearly killed him. Writing to his wife, Clementine, that night, he told her of his innermost feelings on contemplating his extinction. Had the shell fallen a mere twenty yards closer to him, he wrote, it would have been "a good ending to a checkered life, a final gift—unvalued—to an ungrateful country—an impoverishment of the war making power of Britain which no one would ever know or measure or mourn."

In the first few months of Churchill's wartime premiership, one of his hardest tasks and greatest achievements was projecting confidence, even at the blackest of times. In the summer of 1940, during the dangerous, long-drawn-out days and nights of the German invasion and conquest of Belgium, Holland and France and the subsequent German aerial bombardment of Britain, Churchill did not see how Britain could avoid defeat. On returning from Buckingham Palace after becoming Prime Minister—as German forces were breaking through the frontiers of the three northern European nations—he told the detective who was with him: "I hope that it is not too late. I am very much afraid that it is. We can only do our best." An extraordinary feature of his war leadership in those first months, and at other times of crisis, was his ability to hide his doubts and fears from the public. He understood from the outset of his premiership that if he was seen to waiver, public confidence in continuing at war would not be sustained.

The main vehicle by which Churchill sustained that confidence was through his speeches and broadcasts. The twin pillars of his oratory were realism and vision. One complemented the other. When he spoke in Parliament or broadcast to the nation (Parliament having refused to allow his speeches in the House of Commons to be broadcast), he instilled confidence in a way he himself had not anticipated. He made his first public broadcast as Prime Minister at the urging of his predecessor and former opponent, Neville Chamberlain. Those who listened to Churchill's early broadcasts expected to be told, as indeed they were, that times were dangerous and the future dire. What they did not expect to hear, after the stark warnings, was that the Prime Minister looked forward to something very different from a state of siege.

In his first speech in the House of Commons as Prime Minister, on 13 May 1940, while he was still in the process of forming his government, Churchill began by setting out the dangers that were confronting Britain: "I would say to the House, as I said to those who have joined this Government, 'I have nothing to offer but blood, toil, tears and sweat.' We have before us an ordeal of the most grievous kind. We have before us many, many long months of struggle and of suffering. You ask, what is our policy? I will say, It is to wage war, by sea, land and air, with all our might and with all the strength that God can give us; to wage war against a monstrous tyranny, never surpassed in the dark, lamentable catalogue of human crime. This is our policy."

Churchill then went on to present the Members of Parliament with his astonishing vision. "You ask, what is our aim? I can answer in one word: It is victory. Victory at all costs, victory in spite of all terror, victory however long and hard the road may be; for without victory, there is no survival."

The words "a monstrous tyranny" highlighted another facet of Churchill's leadership—his clarity as to the purpose of the war. From the outset of the fighting, when he was First Lord of the Admiralty and a member of Chamberlain's War Cabinet, he was able to convey to the British public something they overwhelmingly felt within themselves: that it was a just war, a war being fought against evil. Even earlier, at the height of the pre-war debate about whether Nazi Germany could, or should, be appeased, Churchill had understood, and conveyed, that what was at stake was the survival of humane values. "War is terrible," he had written on 7 January 1939, "but slavery is worse." From the first months of Nazi rule in Germany, Churchill had spoken out in the House of Commons against the racism of the new regime and the cruel nature of Nazi anti-Semitism. He had argued in 1938 that any appeasement of Germany was a sign not only of British military weakness but also of moral weakness, and that, sooner or later—"and most probably sooner"—both would have to be redressed, since the object of appeasement—to satisfy Hitler by acceding to his territorial demands—would only encourage more and more demands.

When Britain declared war on Germany on 3 September 1939, Churchill spoke in the House of Commons of that moral aspect. He was still a backbencher, awaiting the call—which came after the debate—to join Chamberlain's government. Three days earlier, Germany had invaded Poland and seized the Free City of Danzig. "This is not a question of fighting for Danzig or fighting for Poland," Churchill told the House of Commons. "We are fighting to save the whole world from the pestilence of Nazi tyranny and in defence of all that is most sacred to man. This is no war of domination or imperial aggrandizement or material gain: no war to shut any country out of its sunlight and means of progress. It is a war, viewed in its inherent quality, to establish, on impregnable rocks, the rights of the individual, and it is a war to establish and revive the stature of man."

This speech, reproduced in all the newspapers on the following morning, was a clarion call to those who would have to give up many home comforts to help the war effort and to risk—and sometimes lose—their lives in the battles and aerial bombardments that lay ahead. The speech marked Churchill out as a person—perhaps the only one in government or on its fringes—who saw and clearly expressed the true meaning of Britain's participation in the war. After entering the War Cabinet later that day, as First Lord of the Admiralty, Churchill returned to this theme on 1 October 1939, in his first wartime broadcast, telling his listeners, "We are the defenders of civilization and freedom." In his second broadcast, on 12 November 1939, he recognized the nature of the adversary and spoke with both defiance and hope. "The whole world is against Hitler and Hitlerism," he declared. "Men of every race and clime feel that this monstrous apparition stands between them and the forward move which is their due, and for which the age is ripe. Even in Germany itself there are millions who stand aloof from the seething mass of criminality and corruption constituted by the Nazi Party machine. Let them take courage amid perplexities and perils, for it may well be that the final extinction of a baleful domination will pave the way to a broader solidarity of all the men in all the lands than we could ever have planned if we had not marched together through the fire."

Churchill's clear understanding of the issues at stake enhanced his leadership of the nation even before he became Prime Minister. That vision was conveyed both in speeches and broadcasts to the British public and in secret to his closest colleagues in government. On 18 December 1939, he told the War Cabinet: "We are fighting to establish the reign of law and to protect the liberties of small countries. Our defeat would mean an age of barbaric violence, and would be fatal not only to ourselves, but to the independent life of every small country in Europe." He added that making war might well involve breaches of the rule of law: the issue under discussion was Churchill's request for the violation by British warships of Norwegian territorial waters, to prevent the passage of Swedish iron ore to Germany along the Norwegian coast. But even if such action were to be authorized, Churchill explained that nothing would be done by Britain that would be accompanied by "inhumanity of any kind."

As Prime Minister, Churchill reiterated in his public pronouncements his understanding of the moral nature of the conflict. In his "We shall fight on the beaches" speech of 4 June 1940, he spoke of how "large tracts of Europe and many old and famous States have fallen or may fall into the grip of the Gestapo and all the odious apparatus of Nazi rule." It was that "odious apparatus" against which he fought, and which the British people understood to be the enemy. It was not "Germany" or the German people, but a perversion of all that was decent, humane, modern and constructive in human society. In May 1941, in a message to the American Booksellers Association, he warned that when the minds of nations could be "cowed by the will of one man," then civilization was "broken irreparably." He went on to declare: "A one-man State is no State. It is an enslavement of the soul, the mind, the body of mankind." Hitler's "brute will" had imprisoned or exiled the best of Germany's writers. "Their fault is that they stand for a free way of life. It is a life that is death to meteoric tyrants. So be it. And so it will be."

Even as Britain faced new attacks and new enemies, Churchill was confident that the justness of the cause would prevail. On 12 December 1941, less than a week after Japan had entered the war by attacking American, British and Dutch possession in the Far East and the Pacific, he told the House of Commons that "when we look around us over the sombre panorama of the world we have no reason to doubt the justice of our cause or that our strength and will-power will be sufficient to sustain it." Throughout his five years as war leader, Churchill was able to convey the "justice of our cause"—the Allied cause—and, in conveying it, he reflected the belief of the British public. When, on his eightieth birthday, he was praised as having been the "British lion," he replied with a truer understanding of what his war leadership had been. "It was," he said, "a nation and a race dwelling all around the globe that had the lion's heart. I had the luck to be called upon to give the roar." And, he added: "I also hope that I sometimes suggested to the lion the right places to use his claws."

Knowing the nature of the enemy and making sure the nation had no doubt of the moral aspect of the conflict were important elements in Churchill's war leadership. Another aspect was his understanding of the reality of war. He had no illusions about the dangers war posed both to the fighting men and to the civilians on all sides. That knowledge made his war leadership more humane and more sensitive. In one of his early letters to his wife, written within a year of their marriage in 1908, he wrote: "Much as war attracts me & fascinates my mind with its tremendous situations, I feel more deeply every year—& can measure the feeling here in the midst of arms—what vile & wicked folly & barbarism it all is." During the First World War he had sought to devise policies that would minimize suffering on the battle-field. He had planned the Dardanelles campaign as a means to end the terrible stalemate of trench warfare on the Western Front and to bring the war to a speedier conclusion. He had opposed what he described as Britain's "futile offensives" on the Western Front in 1917, which had culminated in the bloody slaughter at Passchendaele.

During the Second World War Churchill was equally concerned about the human cost of the conflict, and not only to the Allies. At Chequers, after watching a short Royal Air Force film of the bombing of a German city, he commented to those present, "Are we beasts? Are we taking this too far?" But he had no doubt that the war had to be fought; that the struggle was between the forces of democracy and human decency on the one hand and tyranny and dictatorship on the other.

———

No single aspect of Churchill's war leadership was more intricate and more difficult than Britain's relationship with the United States. The burden of this association fell on his shoulders. When Churchill was First Lord of the Admiralty, President Roosevelt had opened up a secret correspondence with him and had shown a genuine concern for the fate of Britain, but Churchill knew that American neutrality—enshrined in the formal legislation of successive Neutrality Acts—and the isolationist pressures that had beset Roosevelt since his first presidential electoral victory in 1933 were barriers to aid from the United States on the scale required.

In the disastrous summer of 1940, with the evacuation of the British Expeditionary Force from Dunkirk (accompanied by a massive loss of equipment) and with the intensification of German bombing of factories and airfields throughout Britain, Churchill and those in the inner circle of government knew the precise details of Britain's weakness on land, sea and air. Despite every effort being made to increase war production, Churchill knew that it was only through a massive contribution by the United States to every facet of Britain's war-making arsenal that Britain could remain effectively at war. From the first to the last days of his premiership, the link to the United States was central to Churchill's war policy. He spent more time and energy in seeking to obtain help from the United States than in any other endeavour. In the First World War, as Minister of Munitions, he had seen at first hand how decisive the arrival of American troops on the Western Front had been. From July 1917 to November 1918 he had worked in tandem with his American opposite number, Bernard Baruch, to secure the raw materials needed to prosecute the war to victory. In the interwar years he had written articles in the American press and broadcast to the United States across the Atlantic, urging Americans to realize that the conflict in Europe between democracy and dictatorship was also their conflict. While he reluctantly accepted that the United States would remain neutral in 1940, he also understood that he had the power to encourage Roosevelt to give Britain the military, naval and air supplies without which the future was bleak.

The British public knew almost nothing of this aspect of Churchill's war leadership. His telegrams to Roosevelt, some 1,300 in all, dealing with every aspect of war strategy and planning, were of the utmost secrecy. Many of the decisions he and Roosevelt reached were equally secret. Without them, Britain's danger would have been far greater. Every aspect of Britain's war-making capacity was affected and enhanced by the American contribution. At the naval battle of Taranto in November 1940, Britain's first major victory over the Italians, the location of the Italian fleet had been a triumph of aerial reconnaissance carried out by a squadron of Glenn Martin photographic reconnaissance aircraft newly arrived in Malta from the United States.

The American dimension was to continue to be central to Churchill's leadership after the entry of the United States into the war in December 1941. Four days after Pearl Harbor, Hitler made his extraordinary mistake—fatal to him in the long run—of declaring war on the United States. Within a month of America's entry into the war, Churchill persuaded Roosevelt to put the defeat of Hitler in Europe as a priority before the defeat of Japan in the Pacific. This decision ensured that the Allied invasion and liberation of Northern Europe would take place at the earliest possible opportunity. Churchill hoped it could be done before the end of 1942, but he accepted the reality that the build-up of American forces in Britain could not be completed until early 1944.

Despite the demands and pressures of war policy, which kept him at his desk and with his colleagues for many hours each day, Churchill was a very visible Prime Minister. His public face was an all-powerful facet of his war leadership, and he made considerable efforts to find time to be seen by the people. He was surprised to discover, at the height of the Blitz, that the Londoners he met within hours of their homes being destroyed, far from cursing him, greeted him with enthusiasm and exhorted him to defeat the enemy. His travels to bombed-out cities proved an enormous boost to public morale. His initially improvised two-finger "V-for-victory" sign became a cause for cheers and enthusiasm amid the devastation of a night bombing raid. Wherever he went, Churchill was acclaimed and cheered (even in 1945, when the crowds who were celebrating victory then went on to the polling booth and cast their votes against his Party). His military secretary and confidant, General Ismay, later recalled an episode on the third day of Churchill's premiership: "I walked with him from Downing Street to the Admiralty. A number of people waiting outside the private entrance greeted him with cries of 'Good luck, Winnie. God bless you.' He was visibly moved, and as soon as we were inside the building, he dissolved into tears. 'Poor people,' he said, 'poor people. They trust me, and I can give them nothing but disaster for quite a long time.'"

Another aspect of Churchill's war leadership that impressed itself on those who saw him at close quarters was his personal example. In his conduct of the war, Churchill set an example for those around him of extreme hard work. His standards were high. "Each night, before I go to bed," he told one of his Private Secretaries, "I try myself by Court Martial to see if I have done something really effective during the day—I don't mean merely pawing the ground, anyone can go through the motions, but something really effective." He was his own severest taskmaster.

The ability of those whom Churchill appointed—their exceptional abilities when crises came—was another aspect of his war leadership. Except in a totalitarian regime, a leader is only as strong as the sum total of those to whom he delegates responsibility. Churchill was a master of the art of delegation—a master and a past master, for his experience in working with subordinates was extensive. No man, however "Churchillian" (as the modern adjective has it), could manage the conduct of a war unless his subordinates were of the highest quality and he had confidence in their abilities. The machinery of war-making between 1940 and 1945 was vast. Every government department devoted its energies in one way or another to the conflict. A massive extension of factories and manufacture focused entirely on war production. Churchill sought the best possible leaders at every level of this national endeavour and supported them in their efforts. On one occasion, answering parliamentary criticisms that he was sluggish, he replied: "I am certainly not one of those who needs to be prodded. In fact, if anything, I am a prod."

There was no more visible aspect of Churchill's war leadership than his daily scrutiny of what was being done across the whole range of execution of war policy. While relying with confidence on those to whom he had delegated the business of war, Churchill followed everything that was being done with a meticulous eye. This rigorous scrutiny had several purposes. First, to ensure that those in whom he had put his trust were carrying out their duties to the highest standard possible. Second, to give praise where it was merited. Praise and encouragement, while not so exciting to the historian as conflict and disagreement, were an essential part of Churchill's "prod." Third, to discover, and rectify, anything he thought was not going well or to suggest a more effective way forward.

Churchill's daily Minutes constituted a stream of questions and questioning about what was being done and how. As he told a member of his Defence Secretariat: "It was all very well to say that everything had been thought of. The crux of the matter was—had anything been done?" To get things done, to ensure that policies that had been decided upon were not only being implemented but carried out expeditiously and effectively, was at the centre of Churchill's daily work. As another member of his Defence Secretariat wrote, "His pugnacious spirit demanded constant action; the enemy must be assailed continuously."

Churchill also had a mastery of detail that enhanced his war leadership over a wide range of complex issues. He had always been interested in the details of policies, however intricate, during his long political career. As First Lord of the Admiralty on the eve of the First World War, he had absorbed himself in the art of flying, had learned to fly (coming within a few hours of his pilot's wings), and had made numerous suggestions for the improvement of flight and the development of aerial warfare. When war came in 1914, he put the resources of the Admiralty behind the evolution of the tank and made many technical suggestions for its development. As

Chancellor of the Exchequer, before establishing pensions for widows and orphans and lowering the age for old age pensions, he studied the actuarial tables to the point where he could converse about them with his most knowledgeable officials.

While at the Admiralty between September 1939 and May 1940, Churchill had made many helpful suggestions about using dummy ships to deceive the Germans, about employing the convoy system to protect British vessels from German submarines, and about many other aspects of naval warfare. When needs became apparent, he made suggestions that often led to substantive and constructive change—as with finding alternate sources of labour to meet the labour shortage in the dockyards, or advancing plans for the placing of radar on ships (before the war he had helped the inventor of radar, Robert Watson-Watt, to obtain a higher priority for his invention). Those closest to Churchill saw his strength in matters of detail. Eric Seal, Churchill's Principal Private Secretary at the Admiralty and later at Downing Street, wrote in a private letter after a stormy meeting in April 1940 about the course of the Norwegian campaign: "Winston is marvellous at picking up all the threads and giving them coherent shape and form."

As Prime Minister, Churchill generated a stream of ideas for weapons, devices, enterprises and initiatives. He was a pioneer in the creation of amphibious tanks (the DD tanks—"Donald Ducks"—that were to come ashore at Normandy). He put forward effective proposals for the urgent repair of bombed airfields during the Battle of Britain. He took a personal interest in enhancing the heavy gun defences of Dover, which was under direct German bombardment from across the Channel. His concern for the public welfare led to probing questions about the availability of gas masks and the construction of air-raid shelters. He took a lead in ensuring that proper compensation would be given to those whose homes had been destroyed by German bombs. He monitored the secrecy and security of military plans with close attention and constant suggestions for improvement.

Weaponry and equipment had always fascinated Churchill: in 1895 his first Intelligence task, given to him by British Military Intelligence, had been to examine at first hand in Cuba the efficacy of the new Spanish rifle being used against the insurgents there. During the Second World War he kept a close watch on all weapons and equipment developments. In May 1942, after studying a plan for artificial harbours—an essential component of the cross-Channel landings two years later—he asked the experts to look into the possibility of floating piers that would "float up and down with the tide." The anchor problem, he added, "must be mastered." And the landing ships "must have a side-flap cut in them and a drawbridge large enough to overreach the moorings of the piers." This was done, and the floating piers became an integral part of the harbours that were built—one for the British and one for the Americans. In April 1944, reading a proposal for the return of adult and child evacuees from Canada and the United States on board the converted troopship *Mauretania*, he wrote: "There must not be more people on this ship, with the women and children, than can be carried in the boats." Attention to detail, to small detail, and yet always with a clear purpose: with the floating piers, to make the cross-Channel landings less dangerous; and with the lifeboats, to ensure the safety of the returning evacuees (aged seven and a half, I was on board that ship).

In all his requests for detailed studies and practical action, Churchill sought positive, hopeful, constructive answers. That, too, was an aspect of his leadership: the optimistic quest. As he wrote at the end of his suggestions for the floating piers: "Let me have the best solutions worked out. Don't argue the matter. The difficulties will argue for themselves."

Churchill had enormous powers, both as Prime Minister and as Minister of Defence. Because he had established a National Government (he called it the "Grand Coalition") and had brought members of all political parties into the highest positions, parliamentary opposition was effectively limited to a handful of malcontents whose dissatisfaction focused more on their exclusion from influence than on specific policies. But Churchill was careful not to abuse the power he had accrued. Reflecting on his new-found authority, he wrote, almost a decade later: "Power, for the sake of lording it over fellow-creatures or adding to personal pomp, is rightly judged base. But power in a national crisis, when a man believes he knows what orders should be given, is a blessing." Twenty-five years earlier, when he had been forced out of office during the Dardanelles campaign, Churchill had written to his wife, "God for a month of power—and a good shorthand writer." In 1940 he had both power and good shorthand writers; and he was to be Prime Minister not for a month but for almost five years.

Central to Churchill's war leadership was his concept of the offensive: the need, as he saw it, to attack whenever possible, even when being attacked. The bombing offensive against Germany was a case in point: in its early stages it was relatively ineffective, and yet, from Churchill's perspective, it constituted something that could be done, and could be seen to be done, to show that Britain did not have to sit back and accept whatever Germany might throw against it. In December 1939, while still at the Admiralty, Churchill had written to a War Cabinet colleague with regard to his own much postponed plan to drop aerial mines into the River Rhine to disrupt German military barge traffic: "The offensive is three or four times as hard as passively enduring from day to day. It therefore requires all possible help in early stages. Nothing is easier than to smother it in the cradle. Yet here perhaps lies safety." That same month Churchill wrote to the First Sea Lord: "An absolute defensive is for weaker forces," and he added: "I could never be responsible for a naval strategy which excluded the offensive principle." He was delighted—"I purred like six cats," he later recalled—when General Wavell sent him a plan for an attack in the Western Desert in November 1940: "At long last we are going to throw off the intolerable shackles of the defensive," he told General Ismay, and added: "Wars are won by superior will-power. Now we will wrest the initiative from the enemy and impose our will on him."

Anything that smacked of passivity on the part of his army commanders incurred Churchill's wrath. Learning at the beginning of November 1941 that nothing "large" was being planned against the German and Italian forces in the Western Desert by Wavell's successor, Churchill wrote to his former Boer War adversary, General Smuts, then a respected voice in Allied military circles: "I dread the idea of this long delay, when, as we know for certain, the enemy is hard pressed for supplies and would be greatly embarrassed by making exertions." He continued: "In war one cannot wait to have everything perfect, but must fight in relation to the enemy's strength and plight. I am appalled at the proposal to remain passive all this time, when the golden opportunity may be lost." Later,

Churchill was to summarize this feeling in a terse comment: “The maxim ‘Nothing avails but perfection’ may be spelt shorter—‘Paralysis.’”

Churchill’s military advisers did not always see his keenness for action as a virtue. In September 1942, during the North African campaign, General Sir Alan Brooke noted in his diary: “It is a regular disease that he suffers from, this frightful impatience to get an attack launched.” But it was an essential feature of his war leadership, and one that enabled him to drive forward the whole machinery of war-making.

In both the military and political spheres, Churchill dreaded prevarication when the need for decisive action seemed to him imperative. In May 1944, confronted by an Anglo-American dispute over how to agree on the role of the Soviet Union in Romania and Greece, he feared that only Stalin would be the beneficiary of Anglo-American hesitations. When Roosevelt suggested the establishment of “consultative machinery” between the Western Allies and the Soviet Union, Churchill replied: “I am much concerned to receive your message. Action is paralyzed if everybody is to consult everybody else about everything before it is taken. Events will outstrip the changing situations in these Balkan regions. Somebody must have the power to plan and act.”

Churchill had always been a believer in the power of the written word—from the time when, as a schoolboy, he would write his mother long letters setting out his requests and point of view and defending his actions. Throughout his political life he was convinced that if he set out an argument clearly, on paper, he might have a chance to influence even the most obdurate of adversaries. These appeals, which are found in the archives of all his political contemporaries from 1900 on, were not always successful, but he believed that the effort should be made and that there should be on record clear, written evidence that, during the war, no stone had been left unturned. One example was his appeal to the Italian dictator, Benito Mussolini, urging him, on 16 May 1940, not to commit Italy as an active ally of Germany.

Churchill had met Mussolini in Rome in 1925, when Churchill was the British Chancellor of the Exchequer, negotiating a settlement of First World War debts with Britain's former Italian ally. In May 1940, Mussolini was poised to attack France—a "stab in the back" that was to outrage British opinion. Churchill desperately wanted to avert bringing Britain into war with a power that could dominate the Mediterranean and threaten the British position in Palestine, Egypt and on the Suez Canal. He wrote in his letter: "Now that I have taken up my office as Prime Minister and Minister of Defence I look back to our meetings in Rome and feel a desire to speak words of goodwill to you as chief of the Italian nation across what seems to be a swiftly-widening gulf. Is it too late to stop a river of blood from flowing between the British and Italian peoples? We can no doubt inflict grievous injuries upon one another and maul each other cruelly, and darken the Mediterranean with our strife. If you so decree it must be so; but I declare that I have never been the enemy of Italian greatness, nor ever at heart the foe of the Italian law-giver."

Churchill then gave Mussolini his assessment of the military situation in Europe: "It is idle to predict the course of the great battles now raging in Europe, but I am sure that whatever may happen on the Continent, England will go on to the end, even quite alone, as we have done before, and I believe with some assurance that we shall be aided in increasing measure by the United States, and, indeed, by all the Americas. I beg you to believe that it is in no spirit of weakness or of fear that I make this solemn appeal, which will remain on record. Down the ages above all other calls comes the cry that the joint heirs of Latin and Christian civilization must not be ranged against one another in mortal strife. Hearken to it I beseech you in all honour and respect before the dread signal is given. It will never be given by us."

Mussolini's son-in-law, the Italian Foreign Minister Count Galeazzo Ciano, found Churchill's appeal "dignified and noble," but Mussolini, excited by the imminent possibility of using Hitler's assault on France to secure for Italy the French regions of Nice and Savoy, ignored it. The result was the embroilment of the Italian forces in a losing war and the destruction, within three years, of Mussolini's Fascist regime.

Another Churchill letter, written at the end of 1940, was to be instrumental in gaining Britain the vital supplies needed from the United States in 1941. The appeal was sent when Britain stood alone and vulnerable, facing German military dominance in Europe, offensive air power, and submarine supremacy. Addressed to President Roosevelt, the letter was written after the Canadian industrialist Arthur Purvis, the head of the British Purchasing Mission in the United States, advised Churchill that Roosevelt would be influenced by a full disclosure of Britain's military, air and naval weaknesses and by a detailed explanation of Britain's urgent requirements. Churchill worked on this letter for two weeks, including his sixty-sixth birthday on 30 November 1940. It was ready to be sent on December 8.

In this letter to Roosevelt, Churchill set out a blunt and forceful assessment of the situation at the time, in all its bleakness and danger for Britain. His mastery of the written word had become an integral, vital part of his war leadership. A central part of the letter read:

> The moment approaches when we shall no longer be able to pay cash for shipping and other supplies. While we will do our utmost, and shrink from no proper sacrifice to make payments across the Exchange, I believe you

> will agree that it would be wrong in principle and mutually disadvantageous in effect if at the height of this struggle Great Britain were to be divested of all saleable assets, so that after the victory was won with our blood, civilization saved, and the time gained for the United States to be fully armed against all eventualities, we should stand stripped to the bone. Such a course would not be in the moral or economic interests of either of our countries. We here should be unable, after the war, to purchase the large balance of imports from the United States over and above the volume of our exports which is agreeable to your tariffs and industrial economy. Not only should we in Great Britain suffer cruel privations, but widespread unemployment in the United States would follow the curtailment of American exporting power . . . Moreover, I do not believe that the Government and the people of the United States would find it in accordance with the principles which guide them to confine the help which they have so generously promised only to such munitions of war and commodities as could be immediately paid for.

This letter to Roosevelt led to a turning point in Britain's ability to remain at war and marked a triumph for a central element of Churchill's war leadership—the use of the written word to persuade and convince. Within a few months, it led to an increased and much more secure American lifeline for Britain—the Lend-Lease arrangement—whereby Britain was sent everything it required from the United States, but did not have to pay until the war was over.

A third communication that illustrates Churchill's use of the written word to try to influence events was sent to the Japanese Foreign Minister, Yosuke Matsuoka, on 2 April 1941. In it Churchill set out the folly of Japan entering the war on the side of the German-Italian Axis, of which Japan was a part, posing a series of questions, each intended to sow doubts about the possibility of Japan emerging victorious from a war with the United States and Britain. The questions, numbered one to eight, started with a blunt reference to Japan's senior partner in the Axis: "Will Germany, without the command of the sea or the command of the British daylight air, be able to invade and conquer Great Britain in the spring, summer or autumn of 1941? Will Germany try to do so? Would it not be in the interests of Japan to wait until these questions have answered themselves?"

The second question dealt with Britain's Atlantic lifeline. "Will the German attack on British shipping be strong enough to prevent American aid from reaching British shores with Britain and the United States transforming their whole industry to war purposes?" Then came a reference to the part that Japan's German and Italian allies might have in determining the position of the United States. "Did Japan's accession to the Triple Pact make it more likely or less likely that the United

States would come into the present war?" And following up from that question: "If the United States entered the war at the side of Great Britain, and Japan ranged herself with the Axis Powers, would not the naval superiority of the two English-speaking nations enable them to dispose of the Axis Powers in Europe before turning their united strength against Japan?"

The fifth question was designed to remind the Japanese of the position of the weakest member of the Axis, Italy, whose fleet had suffered a serious naval defeat at the Battle of Taranto in November 1940, when three of Italy's six battleships had been torpedoed from the air by British pilots (a remarkable precursor of Pearl Harbor). Churchill had three points to make in question form: "Is Italy a strength or a burden to Germany? Is the Italian Fleet as good at sea as on paper? Is it as good on paper as it used to be?"

The sixth question drew the Japanese attention to a fact, the affirmation of which could readily be ascertained by the Japanese Intelligence services. "Will the British air force be stronger than the German Air Force before the end of 1941 and far stronger before the end of 1942?" Question seven went to the heart of the nature of the German occupation regimes in Poland, Norway, Denmark, France, Belgium and Holland (and within a few weeks in Yugoslavia and Greece; and within three months throughout the western Soviet Union): "Will the many countries which are being held down by the

German Army and Gestapo learn to like the Germans more or will they like them less as the years pass by?"

Churchill's final question, which was in two parts, drew attention to the centrality of raw materials in war-making: "Is it true," he asked, "that the production of steel in the United States during 1941 will be seventy-five million tons, and in Great Britain about twelve and a half, making a total of nearly ninety million tons? If Germany should happen to be defeated, as she was last time, will not the seven million tons steel production of Japan be inadequate for a single-handed war?"

Churchill ended his message to Matsuoka: "From the answer to these questions may spring the avoidance by Japan of a serious catastrophe, and a marked improvement in the relations between Japan and the two great sea Powers of the West." To give added weight to his points, Churchill approved a British bombing raid on Berlin the night Matsuoka would be there. As a result, Matsuoka heard Joachim von Ribbentrop—his German opposite number—express confidence in the defeat of Britain while the two men and their staffs were sitting in an air raid shelter listening to the thud, thud, thud of British bombs above them. Five months later, after Matsuoka had been replaced as Foreign Minister, Churchill asked the British ambassador to Japan to show the new Foreign Minister his "warning letter," commenting: "It will read better now than it did then."

Another message that Churchill was keen to see sent,

six months later, was also to Japan. His intention was yet again to try to deter Japan from entering the war. He wanted this particular letter to be sent by Roosevelt, and—a week before Pearl Harbor—gave Roosevelt his ideas of what the message should contain. Basing himself on the experience of Hitler's remilitarization of the Rhineland in 1936, when Britain and France declined to take a firm stand to force the Germans to remove their troops, Churchill urged Roosevelt to send a clear message to Japan of what the consequences of any Japanese aggression against American, British or Dutch possessions in the Far East would be.

"It seems to me," Churchill wrote to the President, "that one important method remains unused in averting war between Japan and our two countries, namely, a plain declaration, secret or public, as may be thought best, that any further act of aggression by Japan"—which had already occupied French Indo-China—"will lead immediately to the gravest consequences. I realize your constitutional difficulties, but it would be tragic if Japan drifted into war by encroachment without having before her fairly and squarely the dire character of a further aggressive step. I beg you to consider whether, at the moment which you judge right, which may be very near, you should not say that 'any further Japanese aggression would compel you to place the gravest issues before Congress,' or words to that effect." Churchill told the President that if he agreed to send such a message to

Japan, in an effort to deter war, Britain "would of course make a similar declaration or share in a joint declaration, and in any case arrangements are being made to synchronize our action with yours."

Churchill ended his letter to Roosevelt on a personal note. "Forgive me, my dear friend, for presuming to press such a course upon you, but I am convinced that it might make all the difference and prevent a melancholy extension of the war." No such American message was sent. At that very moment, the Japanese fleet was already in its final stages of preparation for the torpedo bomb attack on Pearl Harbor and an amphibious landing against the British in Malaya. Churchill did not know these developments. His instinct to make direct appeals, to send messages that were clear and unequivocal, to try to influence the adversary by words and arguments before bombs fell and war broke out was a strong element of his war leadership. He understood the setbacks, the suffering, and the danger to Britain that would follow from any widening of the war, whether by Italy in 1940 or by Japan in 1941.

Face-to-face negotiations were another feature of Churchill's conduct of war policy. Five years after the war he was to coin the word "summit" for what were to become the regular, high-level meetings of Heads of

State and an essential feature of détente. In 1940, among his first acts as Prime Minister, Churchill made three visits to France to meet the French leaders and to attempt to strengthen their will to remain at war. These visits took place as the German army was pushing deep into France. They involved uncomfortable and risky journeys by air, and they meant leaving his command post in London. Churchill believed, however, that the power of personal intervention could be crucial, and that it would be wrong not to try to bolster French resolve by his presence and his arguments. In the end, the overwhelming power of the German army and air force could not be resisted, nor was Churchill able before the fall of Paris to persuade Roosevelt to stiffen French resolve by an American declaration. But the efforts he made to cross over to France, to put his points as forcefully as he could to the French leaders, set a pattern of direct involvement in negotiations at the highest level that became a hallmark of his war leadership.

In August 1941, while the United States was still neutral, Churchill went by sea—on the ill-fated *Prince of Wales*—to the coast of Newfoundland to meet Roosevelt, the first of their many war conferences. Roosevelt never made the journey to Britain. Rather, it was Churchill who made more long journeys to conferences and essential discussions than any other war leader. Later in the war, Churchill met Roosevelt at Casablanca and Malta, first to work out a common war policy, and then a common peace policy in advance of meeting Stalin. Twice Churchill flew to Moscow to talk directly to Stalin. He also travelled to Teheran and Yalta, with Roosevelt, to discuss every aspect of inter-Allied policy with Stalin: the first two meetings of the Big Three.

These journeys, long and arduous even by air, took a great deal out of Churchill physically, but he knew the importance of putting the British case to those who would have the power actually to accede to it. The meetings with Stalin were not a success, despite a considerable effort by Churchill to defer to Stalin's needs. Churchill's repeated efforts to persuade Stalin to allow Poland to have democratic elections after the war appeared to succeed at Yalta, but then Stalin reneged on his promise. With the Red Army the master of Warsaw, there was nothing more that Churchill could do. But he had expended many hours arguing the case for an independent post-war Poland with the Soviet leader, and he had spent as many hours trying to convince the Polish government in London to make concessions. He hoped to get some agreement with the Soviets that would guarantee Polish sovereignty, a Poland that would lose its eastern provinces (its eastern third) to the Soviet Union but would gain a large slice of the industrial region of eastern Germany and the southern half of East Prussia. Churchill put the arguments for some form of territorial compromise with infinite patience—and, when that patience was sorely tried, with considerable irritation—

to the Polish leaders, who had set their hearts against any concessions to the Soviet Union, even in return for the prospect of regaining Polish independence.

Again and again, in face-to-face meetings with foreign leaders, Churchill sought to use his powers of persuasion. Among those with whom he had substantial talks while on his travels were the Polish commander-in-chief General Wladyslaw Anders, the Chinese Nationalist leader, General Chiang Kai-shek, and the two heads of the French national movement, General Charles de Gaulle and General Henri Giraud. Among other leaders to whom Churchill travelled—and it was almost always Churchill who had to make the journeys—was Ismet Inönü, the President of Turkey, whose neutrality Churchill strongly encouraged, to prevent a Turkish accommodation with Germany that would endanger Britain's military position in the Middle East. In seeking to create a post-war Yugoslavia that would not be dominated entirely by the communists, Churchill had talks in Italy with the former ruler of Croatia, Dr. Ivan Subasic, and the Yugoslav Communist leader, Marshal Tito, at whose headquarters, in the German-occupied Balkans, Churchill's son, Randolph, was serving.

At Christmas 1944, learning of the intensity of the civil war that had broken out in Greece even as the German troops were withdrawing, Churchill abandoned his family celebrations and flew to Athens, where, amid the sound of gunfire, he successfully brokered an agreement between the communist and non-communist factions. This was an extraordinary journey, which he undertook in the belief that his personal intervention had a greater chance of success than that of ambassadors and emissaries or telegraphic exhortations from afar.

Another type of journey that Churchill made was also an integral part of his war leadership: the visits to the men and women in the front line of action and danger. In the summer of 1940 he visited the pilots at their airfields during the Battle of Britain and the British coastal areas awaiting invasion. In 1942, after his visit to the sailors of the Home Fleet, the fleet admiral reported: "Your presence with us has been an encouragement and inspiration to us all." In 1943 his appearance at the Roman amphitheatre in Carthage was a tonic for the hundreds of troops crowded into that ancient structure. It was not only British forces Churchill inspired by his presence. When inspecting Czech and Polish troops in Britain, he had words of encouragement that their tormented countries would be liberated. Before the Normandy landings he visited troops of all the nations that would be participating, including the Americans and the Canadians.

After the Normandy landings Churchill twice visited the forward lines, his V-sign, ever-present cigar and cheery grin welcomed with loud cheers. It was a pleasant, unexpected surprise that the Prime Minister had come to see them. "I know how much you enjoy getting near the battle," wrote the commander of an artillery regiment that Churchill visited during his second Normandy excursion, "but also I would like to tell you how tremendously pleased, heartened and honoured every soldier was by your visit. It means very much to them that you should wish to come and see them at work in their gun pits." Churchill was later a witness of the American landings off the South of France, of the fighting in Italy along the River Po, and of the Allied parachute crossing of the Rhine in March 1945. The victorious troops also saw him come among them in Berlin after the German surrender.

Given the enormous complexity of making war, any successful war leader must have the ability to choose subordinates who take responsibility for the actual fighting. Once chosen, the leader must support them in their planning and, when those endeavours fail as a result of weariness or incompetence, the leader must have the strength of purpose to replace them with someone more effective. During the Second World War, to ensure the right men in the right place at the right time sometimes involved hurting many sensitivities of rank, status and popularity. Lord Halifax, Churchill's rival for the premiership in May 1940 and a Tory grandee, was reluctant to give up the Foreign Office, but Churchill had little confidence in his strength of purpose at the centre of the diplomatic web, and sent him instead to be Ambassador to Washington and appointed Anthony Eden in his place. Eden was one of those closest to Churchill. It was to Eden that Churchill confided, in December 1940, about the period six months earlier as France fell and Britain awaited invasion: "Normally I wake up buoyant to face the new day. Then I woke up with dread in my heart." On the day the war in Europe ended, Eden wrote to Churchill: "It is you who have led, uplifted and inspired us through the worst days. Without you this day could not have been."

Those "worst days" had lasted a long time, and put a heavy strain on all those involved in the conduct of the war. Churchill found the physical and mental resources to bear that strain, despite several severe illnesses. He could not replace himself, and followed the advice he gave to one of his secretaries, basing himself on a First World War example: "We must keep working, like the gun horses, till we drop."

Two of the most difficult wartime decisions Churchill had to make in regard to appointments were the removal, first, of General Sir Archibald Wavell and then of General Sir Claude Auchinleck from command in North Africa. In both cases Churchill felt that the initial drive of the commander had faded and that a more energetic commander was needed. As General Ismay recalled after the war, "I think there was a very general impression in Whitehall that Wavell was very tired." After Wavell had been defeated by Rommel, Eden noted, he "had aged ten years in the night." As for Auchinleck, the general himself was anxious to lay down his active command after his sustained exertions, a course of action approved by General Brooke. Those not in possession of the facts and the recommendations reaching Churchill felt that the dismissals of Wavell and Auchinleck were petty or vindictive. But in both cases he acted on advice and on his belief that change was in the immediate and urgent interest of the prosecution of the war.

The third officer to be given the crucial North Africa command was General Bernard Montgomery (following the death in a plane crash of the general actually chosen to succeed Auchinleck). Montgomery had impressed Churchill in 1940, during the Prime Minister's inspection of coastal defences on the eve of what was thought to be a German invasion, by his pugnacious attitude to what could be done if German troops were seen offshore (if they were able to reach the shore, Montgomery was prepared to consider the use of poison gas against them). When Montgomery was appointed to command in the Western Desert, Churchill wrote to his wife that, in the new commander, "we have a highly competent, daring, energetic soldier, well-acquainted with desert warfare." Clementine Churchill had heard that Montgomery had created animosities in military circles: "If he is disagreeable to those about him," Churchill replied, "he is also disagreeable to the enemy." And to Montgomery himself,

Churchill soon sent a message of praise for the fighting in North Africa: "Tell him how splendid we all think his work has been."

It was not only the military sphere that Churchill closely monitored. He was always quick to encourage those whose work he regarded highly. At the centre of all strategic deception plans (including "The Man Who Never Was" in the Mediterranean deception in 1943, and the bogus First United States Army Group deception leading the Germans to expect the 1944 Normandy landings to come from elsewhere), Churchill had full confidence in the innocuously named London Controlling Centre and its chief, Colonel John Bevan. Bevan's professionalism and attention to detail required no prodding from Churchill and received none. Another of those whose work Churchill admired was the British diplomat Ronald Campbell, who had been at his side during his dramatic visits to France in June 1940. On receiving a report from Campbell, then the senior British diplomat in Belgrade, in April 1941, while Campbell was working to drive a wedge between Yugoslavia's pro-German Regent, Prince Paul, and those Ministers in the Yugoslav government known to be hostile to Germany, Churchill telegraphed Campbell approvingly: "Continue to pester, nag and bite. Demand audiences. Don't take NO for an answer." This advice was very much Churchill's own prescription for himself, and he was pleased to see it reflected in the actions of another. Nor did he neglect to praise

Campbell for what he regarded as a remarkable mission. "Greatly admire all you have done so far," he wrote. "Keep it up by every means that occur to you."

"Continue to pester, nag and bite" summed up Churchill's own method of war leadership. To one of his commanders-in-chief he had a further exortation: "Improvise and dare."

One of the more contentious of Churchill's wartime appointments was that of Lord Beaverbrook, a wealthy Canadian businessman who had arrived in Britain before the First World War, created a newspaper empire, and become a newspaper Baron in the process. Beaverbrook was regarded by many in public life as an opportunist and a schemer. Churchill knew him well and recognized great virtues among great faults. When Churchill first wanted to bring Beaverbrook into the government in April 1940, Neville Chamberlain had said no. But Churchill, aware of the terrible shortage of aircraft, and of fighter aircraft in particular, judged that the ruthlessness that marked Beaverbrook out in the newspaper world, and even in his personal relationships, could be used to vital effect in accelerating the manufacture of aircraft when Britain's need was dire and Germany's destructive powers were at their height. "Now that the war is coming so close," Churchill wrote to Beaverbrook on 24 May 1940, "the object must be to prepare the largest number of aircraft"—and this Beaverbrook did, as Minister of Aircraft Production. Other government departments found Beaverbrook's methods dictatorial and rapacious, but they served the need of the hour, and Churchill supported him. "Your work during the crisis at MAP [the Ministry of Aircraft Production] in 1940," Churchill wrote to him later in the war, "played a decisive part in our salvation."

Beaverbrook also provided Churchill with the moral support of his presence and energy at several moments of crisis. Twenty-five years earlier, when Churchill had left Britain and the turmoil of politics to seek active military duty on the Western Front, Beaverbrook, who was then Chief Canadian Press Representative at the Front, had shown Churchill the hand of friendship and encouraged him not to despair of a return to political life and influence on war policy. In the days immediately before Churchill became Prime Minister, when the British naval initiative in Norway was foiled by the Germans, and Churchill was much criticized, Beaverbrook had again been supportive. Twice in the early months of Churchill's war premiership, first at the fall of France, and then at the moment of the terrible decision to bombard the French fleet at Oran to prevent it from falling into German hands, Beaverbrook had been at Churchill's side. On one occasion, when Churchill could not see how the situation in France might be redeemed, he spent the night at Beaverbrook's house in London, talking through the crisis and gaining strength from his friend's determination. The choice of senior colleagues was often a two-way exchange of this sort:

Churchill could inspire them to great efforts and achievements, and they could give Churchill support and confidence when he had his moments of doubt.

Among his choice of officials to do the essential work he depended on was his long-time friend Professor Frederick Lindemann (whom Churchill created Baron Cherwell during the war). From the earliest days of Churchill's war premiership, he gave Lindemann access to the most secret aspects of the war, with a view to using his mathematical and statistical expertise to examine the information reaching him from all government departments in the sphere of production, manufacture, and the projected needs and performances of every facet of Britain's war needs. As head of Churchill's Statistical Branch, Lindemann and the small team working under him provided Churchill with an independent assessment of the working of the war machine. On an almost daily basis during the times of greatest crisis, Churchill would send Lindemann his requests. A typical one, dated 24 May 1940, read: "Let me have on one sheet of paper a statement about the Tanks. How many have we got with the Army? How many of each kind are being made each month? How many are there with manufacturers? What are the forecasts? What are the plans for heavier Tanks?"

Lindemann and his team provided Churchill with the information he needed to enable him to follow up with the relevant government departments and, where necessary, to accelerate action. Sometimes Churchill felt the need to stimulate Lindemann himself to greater efforts. On 3 June 1940, he minuted to him: "You are not presenting me as I should like every few days, or every week with a short clear statement of the falling off or improvement in munitions production. I am not able to form a clear view unless you do this."

Not only did Lindemann give Churchill the ability to look with an independent eye on the workings of production and manufacture but he also undertook to supervise and accelerate work on new inventions and to examine—using material provided through Enigma—the actual strength of the German air force. The two men were good friends. Lindemann spent almost every weekend with Churchill and travelled with him to a number of overseas conferences. As one of the few people with constant access to the Prime Minister, he was a source of strength in times of setback and difficulty.

Other officials, less well known than Lindemann, played their part in ensuring the smooth working of the machine and in overcoming difficulties. Each of them was an integral part of the complex mosaic that made up Churchill's war leadership. In Washington Arthur Purvis worked tirelessly to secure the munitions of war and other war supplies desperately needed by Britain. His daily telegraphic exchanges with London and his ability to persuade the United States administration—including Roosevelt's closest advisers—to fulfill Britain's urgent needs have no place in most of the history books of the period, or indeed in most of the Churchill biographies, but for the first year of Churchill's premiership Purvis was a central pivot in ensuring the success of Churchill's determination to remain at war and to wage war effectively. At the very moment when Churchill sought to reward Purvis with a knighthood, the Canadian was killed in a plane crash while on his way to join Churchill and Roosevelt in Newfoundland.

Among the other little-known pillars of Churchill's war leadership was General M.G.H. Barker, whom Churchill had appointed Vulnerable Points Adviser in August 1940 as the threat of invasion intensified. As with several of those whose work was crucial at a time of danger, Churchill gave instructions that Barker "should work under me in my capacity as Minister of Defence." This authority enabled Barker to ensure that troops, weapons and equipment were sent to the areas most vulnerable to German invasion at any given date and at the shortest notice—depending on the state of the tide and the moon and on Intelligence indications—without becoming ensnared in conflicting interests of a dozen different government departments. Churchill scrutinized all Barker's proposals and endorsed them without complaint, noting on most "Proceed as proposed."

Another officer Churchill brought within his own orbit as Minister of Defence and provided with research facilities only a few miles from Chequers was Major Millis Jefferis. Churchill had first noted Jefferis's abilities a month before he became Prime Minister, when Jefferis had blown up key railway bridges behind German lines in Norway. In giving Jefferis considerable powers and authority in August 1940, Churchill minuted, "I regard this Officer as a singularly capable and forceful man who should be brought forward to a higher position." When the Army Council resisted Jefferis's advancement in rank before his time (he was 150th on the list of majors in the Royal Engineers), Churchill wrote in protest to the Chief of the Army Staff, "Surely it is important to bring able men forward in war time, instead of referring entirely to seniority."

Jefferis was to work for the rest of the war as head of a special defence establishment, directly under the Minister of Defence. This establishment was the scene of extensive rocket research throughout the war. From time to time Jefferis took his rockets and bombs to Chequers to demonstrate them to the Prime Minister. By the end of the war, he had been promoted to major-general and knighted.

Churchill's ability to find, encourage and sustain individuals who he knew would make a significant contribution to the war effort was an important feature of his war leadership. One of the most remarkable of these characters, for whom Churchill had to fight tenaciously, was a retired major-general, Percy Hobart, who before the war had been one of the main figures in the development of tank warfare. In 1936 Hobart had gone to see Churchill—then in the political wilderness—in search of a more vigorous tank policy. Hobart, who was unpopular among the officials in the War Office, had been retired in March 1940 and refused reinstatement. In October 1940 he was serving as a private in the Home Guard. Churchill was surprised that Hobart's talents were not being used and pressed for his re-employment. That was not an easy task, particularly when the Chief of the Imperial Staff, Field Marshal Sir John Dill, informed Churchill that Hobart had on various occasions during his military career been "impatient, quick tempered, hot headed, intolerant and inclined to see things as he wished them to be instead of as they were."

Churchill was not deterred, writing to Dill about Hobart in a Minute that resonates with the flavour of Churchill's mind and perceptions:

> I am not at all impressed by the prejudices against him in certain quarters. Such prejudices attach frequently to persons of strong personality and original view. In this case General Hobart's original views have been only too tragically borne out. The neglect by the General Staff even to devise proper patterns of tanks before the war has robbed us of all the fruits of this invention. These fruits have been reaped by the enemy, with terrible consequences. We should therefore remember that this was an officer who had the root of the matter in him, and also vision . . .

> We are now at war, fighting for our lives, and we cannot afford to confine Army appointments to persons who have excited no hostile comment in their career. The catalogue of General Hobart's qualities and defects might almost exactly have been attributed to most of the great commanders of British history. Marlborough was very much not the conventional soldier, carrying with him the goodwill of the Service. Cromwell, Wolfe, Clive, Gordon, and in a different sphere Lawrence, all had very close resemblance to the characteristics set down as defects. They had other qualities as well, and so I am led to believe has General Hobart.

This was a time, Churchill added, "to try men of force and vision and not to be exclusively confined to those who are judged thoroughly safe by conventional standards." As Churchill wished, Hobart was re-employed. Just as Jefferis made a substantial contribution to the weaponry of war, so Hobart designed an array of armoured vehicles (known as "Hobart's funnies") that made a major contribution to the Normandy landings.

There were others in Churchill's confidence whose judgment he trusted and whose presence he welcomed during times of crisis, men who were to be a sustaining part of his war leadership. One was Desmond Morton, his liaison with governments in exile, including the Poles, Dutch and Belgians, and with De Gaulle. Morton was also a link between Churchill and the Intelligence services. As

Secretary of State for War, Churchill had appointed Morton to his first Intelligence post in 1919. Even closer to Churchill was Brendan Bracken, a political ally during the anti-appeasement battle, whom Churchill appointed Minister of Information. At the many weekends spent at Chequers, when work and relaxation combined, Lindemann and Bracken were often overnight guests, able to enhance the free flow of ideas that so often led to action. Churchill also gained strength from two Americans in London, both of whom were frequently with him at Chequers and on his journeys to the bombed cities: Roosevelt's emissary, Averell Harriman, and the American Ambassador, Gilbert Winant. Harriman accompanied Churchill on several of his overseas journeys and provided a link between Churchill and Roosevelt over a wide range of military and international needs. "I have made great friends with him," Churchill wrote of Harriman in a private letter to his son, Randolph, "and have the greatest regard for him. He does all he can to help us."

Forming an indispensable adjunct and support to Churchill's war leadership were the Ministers he appointed to his Cabinet, as well as the Ministers of State and Ministers-Resident overseas. Several of these Ministers were brought in by him from outside the political world. He sought, and found, those who were able to carry out most effectively the departmental tasks he had to delegate, and he delegated with confidence, regularly scrutinizing their work but seldom feeling the need to interfere in it. Later he wrote of Lord Leathers, his Minister of War Transport—a post Churchill established in May 1941 to amalgamate the often conflicting needs of the Ministry of Shipping and the Ministry of Transport: "Leathers was an immense help to me in the conduct of the war. It was very rarely that he was unable to accomplish the hard tasks I set. Several times, when all staff and departmental processes had failed to solve the problems of moving an extra division or trans-shipping it from British to American ships, or of meeting some other need, I made a personal appeal to him, and the difficulties seemed to disappear as if by magic."

Another Minister whose work sustained Churchill throughout the war was Oliver Lyttelton (later Lord Chandos). First as a member of Churchill's Defence Secretariat at the Ministry of Defence, in charge of all liaison with munitions production, then as Minister of Trade, and finally as Minister of State in the Middle East, he brought his formidable qualities as an industrialist to the task of war organization. Churchill's son-in-law Duncan Sandys was also a pillar of strength, serving first on the Defence Secretariat as liaison with the Home Defence and Air Raid Precautions departments, and later as the person in charge of ascertaining the facts about German flying-bomb and rocket-bomb research and devising countermeasures. It was the Chiefs of Staff who suggested Sandys for the post, and Churchill accepted their advice.

The qualities of Churchill's war leadership were shown in his appointments, and they were sustained by the men he appointed.

One essential feature of Churchill's war leadership was his ability to act with decision and, if necessary, with ruthlessness. During the interwar years the Turkish leader Kemal Ataturk—who had played a crucial part in the Turkish defences at Gallipoli—noted in the margin of his copy of Churchill's First World War memoirs, against a passage describing the lack of decision-making at a crucial moment of the Gallipoli campaign, the Turkish saying: "History is ruthless to those who lack ruthlessness." Did Churchill possess such ruthlessness? In a letter to the Prime Minister, Asquith, in May 1915, as her husband was being forced to stand down from the Admiralty, Clementine Churchill wrote: "If you throw Winston overboard you will be committing an act of weakness and your Coalition Government will not be as formidable a War machine as your present Government. Winston may in your eyes & in those with whom he has to work have faults, but he has the supreme quality which I venture to say very few of your present or future Cabinet possess, the power, the imagination, the deadliness to fight Germany."

How far did such "deadliness" show itself in the Second World War? In June 1940 the War Cabinet authorized the detention without trial of tens of thousands of German-born "enemy aliens," fearing they might serve as a pro-German fifth column in the event of an invasion. Many of those arrested were German opponents of Nazism who had found refuge in Britain. Others were German Jews, recent refugees from Nazi racial prosecution, but the prospect of invasion seemed so imminent that there was no time to examine individual cases. One of those arrested and interned was a German-Jewish refugee, Eugen Spier, who from 1936 to 1939 had helped finance the Focus, an all-Party group that Churchill set up to discuss the Nazi danger and to make it more widely known. These swift and widespread internments have been commented on as an example of Churchill's ruthlessness. Less publicized is Churchill's wish to avoid these draconian measures. "Many enemy aliens," he told the War Cabinet as the plan was going ahead, "had a great hatred of the Nazi regime, and it was unjust to treat our friends as our foes." Churchill put forward another idea, to form all able-bodied anti-Nazi aliens into a Foreign Legion for training and eventual use as garrison troops overseas, possibly in Iceland, which Britain had just occupied. But the War Cabinet insisted on internment, and Churchill had no veto on its decisions and deferred to the arguments of the Minister responsible, Sir John Anderson—formerly a member of Neville Chamberlain's Cabinet—who insisted that the internment was essential and urgent.

One of the most ruthless British wartime acts, certainly in terms of loss of life, was the decision in July 1940 to open fire on the warships of the French fleet then at anchor in the French North African port of Oran, after the Germans had insisted, as part of the Franco-German Armistice agreement, that all French warships be transferred to German control. Desperate to prevent these ships from becoming part of a German invasion fleet, Churchill offered the French admiral the choice of scuttling them or sailing them to a British or a neutral port for the duration of the war. If the admiral refused, Churchill decided that the ships would have to be sunk or disabled. For much of July 3, negotiations with the French admiral continued, but when it became clear, from an intercepted French naval signal, that the admiral would continue to refuse the British terms, the British warships outside Oran opened fire and more than 1,250 French sailors, Britain's allies of only a few weeks earlier, were killed.

For Churchill, a lifelong friend of the French people, this course was horrendously difficult to take, although dictated by the urgent needs of war and survival. It had one unexpected and beneficial result: it convinced President Roosevelt—despite the belief of his ambassador, Joseph Kennedy (the father of John F. Kennedy), to the contrary—that the British really were determined to fight on, and that any war material sent to Britain would not be allowed to fall into German hands as a result of an armistice. It had been his hope, Churchill told the House of Commons during the Oran debate, "that our terms would be accepted without bloodshed." When Churchill finished his statement, in which he told the House, "We shall not fail in our duty, however painful," the whole House rose to its feet to cheer. It was the first such demonstration of his premiership. Churchill wept, and as he left the chamber he was heard to say to a fellow Member: "This is heartbreaking to me."

Churchill's ruthlessness was tempered with compassion. Throughout the war, Churchill was disturbed and distressed when it came to high casualty lists, whether of soldiers or civilians. At the time of the Normandy landings he dreaded a heavy loss of life and did his utmost to devise means of minimizing the casualties among the landing forces. Before the landings he confided to an American visitor, John J. McCloy, Roosevelt's Under-Secretary for War: "If you think I'm dragging my feet, it is not because I can't take casualties; it is because I am afraid of what those casualties will be." Churchill went on to explain to McCloy that many of his contemporaries had been killed in what he called the "hecatombs" of the First World War, and that he himself was "a sort of 'sport' in nature's sense as most of his generation lay dead at Passchendaele and the Somme." Churchill added: "An entire generation of potential leaders had been cut off and Britain could not afford the loss of another generation."

During the pre-Normandy preparations, Churchill was uneasy about the heavy Anglo-American bombing of railway marshalling yards and railway bridges in northern France because of the high French and Belgian civilian casualties. When the Supreme Commander of the Allied Expeditionary Forces, General Dwight D. Eisenhower, insisted that this bombing was essential if the landings were to go ahead, Churchill put the matter to Roosevelt. Churchill stressed that the civilian casualties, sometimes several hundred in a single raid, were too high and that some limit should be set, per raid. If the estimate of civilian deaths was above a certain number, Churchill advised, the raid should not take place. Roosevelt declined to set any limit, however, and the raids continued. In all, more than five thousand French and Belgian civilians were killed, but the effective disruption of German communications in a great arc around the beachhead was a boon to the Allied landings—and to the eventual liberation of France and Belgium. Churchill commented to Air Chief Marshal Sir Arthur Tedder, the British air commander-in-chief and Eisenhower's deputy, "You are piling up an awful load of hatred;" but, with Roosevelt's intervention, Churchill's hesitations had to be set aside.

In 1940 Churchill had authorized the bombing of German cities—then on a small scale—as the one means of waging war on Germany, whose armies were masters of Europe. As the British, and later Anglo-American, bombing raids intensified, he was uneasy at the high civilian casualties and became an advocate of targeted strategic bombing, as opposed to "terror" bombing. The subsequently controversial Anglo-American bombing raid on Dresden was approved not by Churchill but by the British Deputy Prime Minister, Clement Attlee, during Churchill's absence on his way to the Yalta Conference at the beginning of February 1945. When Churchill was given the first detailed account of the raid, he was appalled, minuting to the Chiefs of Staff Committee: "It seems to me that the moment has come when the question of bombing of German cities simply for the sake of increasing the terror, although under other pretexts, should be reviewed." The destruction of Dresden, Churchill added, "remains a serious query against the conduct of Allied bombing. I am of the opinion that military objectives must henceforth be more strictly studied." Only later did he learn that it was an urgent Soviet request to disrupt accelerated German troop movements through Silesia that had led to the bombing raid on Dresden.

Reflecting on the first half of the twentieth century, and on the destructiveness of aerial bombardment by all sides during the Second World War, Churchill commented in 1953: "On the whole I would rather have lived through our lot of troubles than any of the others, though I must place on record my regret that the human race ever learned to fly." The pervasiveness of aerial destruction, and the destructiveness of all forms of warfare, was, despite Churchill's hesitations and those of many others, a cruel but integral part of modern war. Churchill had seen the horrors of war at first hand and had written much about it since his time as a soldier at the end of the nineteenth century. J.M. Keynes called *The World Crisis*—Churchill's history of the First World War—"a tractate against war."

The preservation and enhancement of democracy was an integral part of Churchill's war leadership, a vision of the world that would follow an Allied victory. Upholding democratic values, both in Britain and throughout post-war Europe, where democracies had been submerged by Fascism and Nazism, became a task and a call. "It was Parliament," Churchill told his fellow parliamentarians—many of whom were serving officers—that constituted "the shield and expression of democracy," and it was in Parliament that "all grievances or muddles or scandals, if such there be," should be debated.

Churchill recognized the dangers to Britain's war effort of the sort of parliamentary criticism, within the framework of Britain's parliamentary democracy, that might give comfort to the enemy. With this aspect of free speech in mind, he told the House of Commons in 1942, during a no-confidence motion that was decisively defeated: "If democracy and Parliamentary institutions are to triumph in this war, it is absolutely necessary that Governments resting on them shall be able to act and dare, that the servants of the Crown shall not be harassed by nagging and snarling, that enemy propaganda shall not be fed needlessly out of our own hands, and our reputation disparaged and undermined throughout the world."

At the beginning of 1942, while Churchill was in Bermuda on the way back to Britain after his first wartime visit to the United States, he set out in a public speech his thoughts on the importance of democracy, both in regard to the war then at its height and as a pointer to how the post-war world ought to look. "These ideas of parliamentary government," he said, "of the representation of the people upon franchises, which extend as time goes on, and which in our country have reached the complete limits of universal suffrage, these institutions and principles constitute at this moment one of the great causes which are being fought out in the world." Churchill had no illusions about the weaknesses of democracy, but, as he went on to explain: "With all their weakness and with all their strength, with all their faults, with all their virtues, with all the criticism that may be made against them, with their many shortcomings, with lack of foresight, lack of continuity of purpose, or pressure only of superficial purpose, they nevertheless assert the right of the common people—the broad mass of the people—to take a conscious and effective share in the government of their country."

Churchill was to return to this theme in public, and in the House of Commons, on several occasions during the war. When, in August 1944, he was in Italy, he was asked to advise on the system of government to replace Mussolini's Fascist regime, which had ruled Italy for more than twenty years. "It is said," Churchill told the Italian people, "that the price of freedom is eternal vigilance," and he went on to ask rhetorically, "What is freedom?" There were, he answered, "one or two quite simple, practical tests by which it can be known in the modern world in peace conditions," and he set out those tests in the form of seven questions that the Italian people should answer if they wanted to know whether they had replaced fascism by freedom:

> Is there the right to free expression of opinion and of opposition and criticism of the Government of the day?
>
> Have the people the right to turn out a Government of which they disapprove, and are constitutional means provided by which they can make their will apparent?
>
> Are their courts of justice free from violence by the Executive and from threats of mob violence, and free from all association with particular political parties?
>
> Will these courts administer open and well-established laws, which are associated in the human mind with the broad principles of decency and justice?
>
> Will there be fair play for poor as well as for rich, for private persons as well as for Government officials?

> Will the rights of the individual, subject to his duties to the State, be maintained and asserted and exalted?
>
> Is the ordinary peasant or workman, who is earning a living by daily toil and striving to bring up a family, free from the fear that some grim police organization under the control of a single Party, like the Gestapo, started by the Nazi and Fascist parties, will tap him on the shoulder and pack him off without fair or open trial to bondage or ill-treatment?

As much as the Atlantic Charter of August 1941, which had been drafted by Roosevelt and the Americans but signed also by Churchill, these questions were a mark and proof of the ultimate objective of Churchill's war leadership: faith in democracy, the need to preserve democracy, and the hope of returning democracy to those countries that had been deprived of it by the victories of totalitarianism. As Churchill told the House of Commons in December 1944, four months after his questions to the Italian people and at a time when democracy had come under grave threat in liberated Greece in the form of a civil war: "Democracy is no harlot to be picked up in the street by a man with a Tommy gun. I trust the people, the mass of the people, in almost any country, but I like to make sure that it is the people and not a gang of bandits from the mountains or from the countryside who think that by violence they can overturn constituted authority, in some cases ancient Parliaments, Governments and States."

It was to avert a Communist takeover in Greece, and the replacement of a tyranny dictated from Berlin by one dictated from Moscow, that Churchill had flown to Greece at Christmas 1944 and negotiated between the Greek forces led by Archbishop Damaskinos and those rival Greek forces directed from afar by the Soviet Union. Churchill's presence made a powerful impact, as did his advocacy, and agreement was reached whereby Greece's democratic system would be maintained. Churchill had also opposed the creation in Greece of a dictatorship of the right, which was one of the possibilities being mooted in London. "I do not like setting up dictators as a result of using British troops in action," he wrote on the day before his arrival in Athens. "I am a believer in constitutional processes. Of course if the Greeks agree among themselves that the Archbishop is the best man to head the new government as Prime Minister it might make a very good solution; but to make him dictator of Greece to get round an awkward political corner is entirely contrary to the guiding principles on which I act."

Seven months after his dramatic journey to Athens, Churchill's faith in democracy was borne out by events closer to home. In July 1945 the Conservative Party in Britain was defeated at the General Election, and Churchill, who in May 1945 had become Prime Minister of a Conservative caretaker government following Hitler's defeat and the ending of the all-Party coalition, was out of office. He accepted the verdict of the electorate, telling one of those who spoke of the "ingratitude" of the British people: "I wouldn't call it that. They have had a very hard time." Following the election defeat, Churchill became Leader of the Opposition and, working within the parliamentary system he had espoused all his life, led his Party to victory in 1951. One of the underlying strengths of his war leadership—his determination to see the victory of democracy over dictatorship—served to bring him back to power with another full national agenda, including an attempt to avert a nuclear war by means of a renewal of conferences and discussions at the highest level with Stalin's successors. As he told a group of senators and congressmen in Washington in June 1954: "Communism is a tyrant but meeting jaw to jaw is better than war." His war leadership had confirmed his belief that war, however justified it might be, was for the combatants (in his phrase of 1909) "vile wicked folly & a barbarism," that statesmen had a duty to try to avert.

Between 1936 and 1939 Churchill had believed that a European war could be averted by the unity and strength of all threatened states. That unity had not been created, nor had those who were most in danger built up sufficient armaments to be able to deter an aggressor by themselves. From 1946, when he spoke at Fulton, Missouri, about the "Iron Curtain," Churchill used his experience of the pre-war years, and his knowledge of how hard it had been in wartime to secure victory as a result of pre-war neglect, to advocate direct talks with the new adversary, the Soviet Union. These discussions should be held at the highest level, he said, and be based on Anglo-American (and, in due course, European) unity and strength, to secure an amelioration of international tensions. In both war and peace his leadership bore the hallmarks of clarity of vision, strength of purpose, and faith in the ultimate victory of decency and goodwill.

The comments of those who saw Churchill in action at close quarters during the war give an insight into his leadership qualities during those five hard years. From these contemporary remarks, made in the first year and a half of his premiership when the dangers were greatest—remarks that Churchill himself never saw—I have chosen sixteen that reflect his qualities in all their variety, and mark out his leadership as something rare among the twentieth-century war leaders: "galvanizing people at all levels," "a manifestly humane person," "no rigidity of mind," "nothing can frighten him," "a gentle, almost paternal smile," "ready as always with confident advice," "ceaseless industry," "strength, resolution, humour, readiness to listen," "a wonderful tonic," "enough courage for everybody," "really he has got guts," "in wonderful spirits, and full of offensive plans," "innately lovable and generous," "amazing grasp of detail," "full of the most marvellous courage, considering the burden he is bearing," and, in tandem with this last and at the centre of all Churchill's leadership struggles and decisions, "carrying the heaviest burden of responsibility any man has ever shouldered."

Reflecting towards the end of his life on her father's war leadership, Churchill's daughter Mary summed up a nation's feelings when she wrote to him: "I owe you what every Englishman, woman & child does—Liberty itself."

Note on Sources

The material in this lecture is taken from my book *Churchill: A Life*, as well as from the six volumes of the Churchill biography, *Winston S. Churchill*, covering the years 1914 to 1965, and the eleven document volumes covering the years 1914 to 1941, which I have published over the past thirty years.

Index